THE UKULELE

4 Chord Songbook

PLAY 50 GREAT SONGS WITH JUST 4 EASY CHORDS!

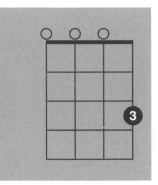

C

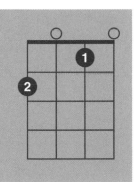

F

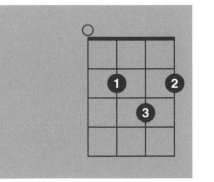

G

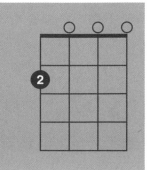

Am

ISBN 978-1-4950-1125-2

HAL•LEONARD®
CORPORATION

7777 W. BLUEMOUND RD. P.O. BOX 13019 MILWAUKEE, WI 53213

Visit Hal Leonard Online at
www.halleonard.com

4 Chord Songbook

PLAY 50 GREAT SONGS WITH JUST 4 EASY CHORDS!

Contents

Candle in the Wind

Words and Music by Elton John and Bernie Taupin

First note

Verse
Gently, reflectively

1. Good-bye, Nor - ma Jean, _____ though I nev - er knew you _____ at all,
2. *See additional lyrics*

you had the grace to hold your-self _____ while those a - round _ you crawled. _

_____ They crawled out of the wood - work

and they whis-pered in - to _____ your brain. _ They set you _ on the tread -

- mill _____ and they made you change _ your name. _____

Chorus

And it seems to me __ you lived your __ life __ like a

can - dle in __ the wind, _____ nev - er know-ing who to cling _

__ to when the rain set in. __ And I

would have liked __ to have known you, but I was just ____ a kid. Your

can - dle burned _ out long be - fore __ your

leg-end ev - er did. _____

Verse

3. Good-bye, Nor - ma Jean, _____ though I nev - er knew you __ at all,

you had the grace to hold your-self ____ while those a - round __ you crawled. __

__ Good - bye, Nor - ma Jean,

from the young man in the twen - ty - sec - ond row ____

who sees you as some-thing more than sex - ual, _____ more than

just our Mar - i - lyn Mon - roe. And it

Chorus

seems to me ____ you lived ____ your life ____ like a can - dle in ____ the wind, ____ nev - er know - ing who to cling ____ to when the rain ____ set in. ____ And I would have liked ____ to have known you, but I was just ____ a kid. Your can - dle burned ____ out long be - fore ____ your leg - end ev - er did. ____ I

Outro

would have liked ___ to have known you, whoa, ___ but I ___

___ was just a kid. ___ Your can - dle burned ___ out long ___

___ be - fore ___ your leg - end ev - er did. ___

rit.

Additional Lyrics

2. Loneliness was tough, the toughest role you ever played.
   Hollywood created a superstar and pain was the price you paid.
   Even when you died, oh, the press still hounded you.
   All the papers had to say was that Marilyn was found in the nude.

Brown Eyed Girl

Words and Music by Van Morrison

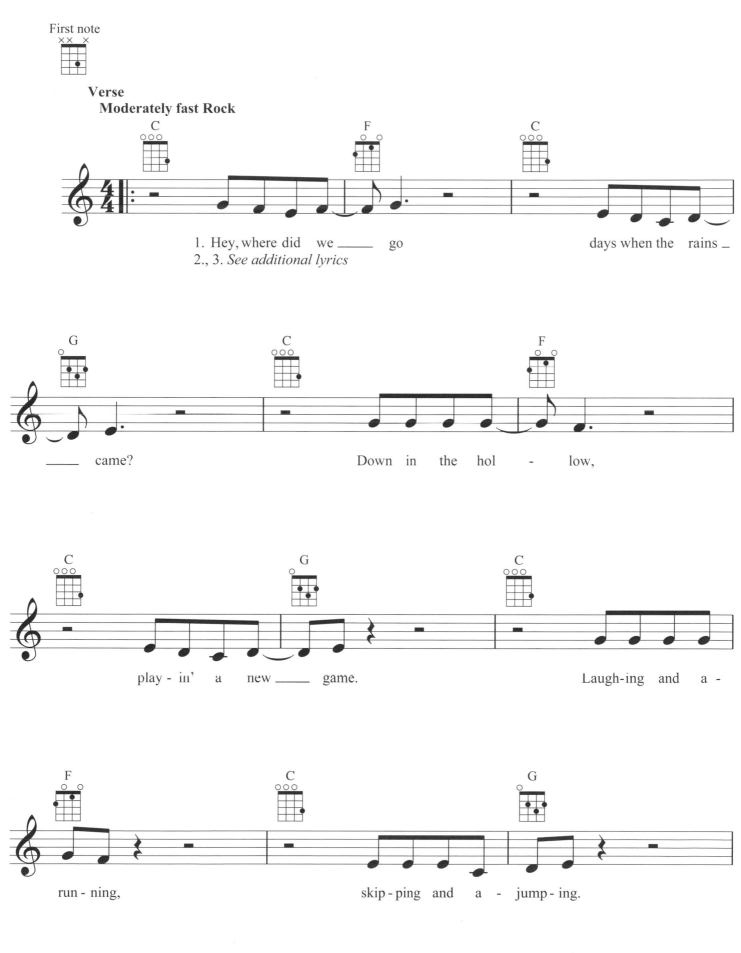

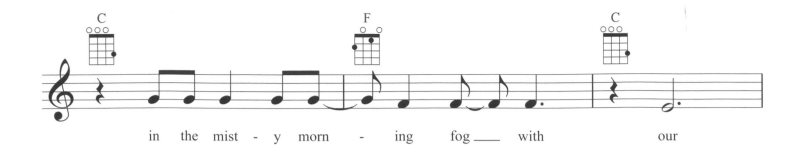

in the mist - y morn - ing fog ____ with our

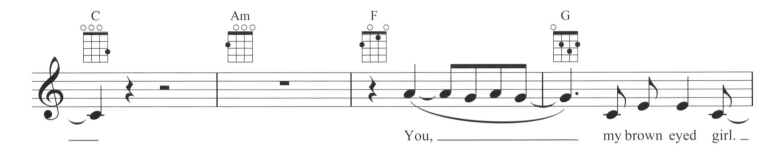

hearts a - thump - in', and you, ____ my brown eyed girl. ____

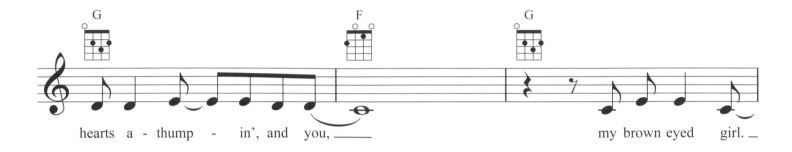

You, ____ my brown eyed girl. ____

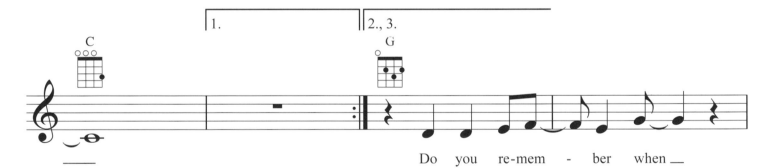

____ Do you re-mem - ber when ____

Chorus

we used to sing: ____ Sha, la, ____ la, la, ____ la, la, ____ la, la, ____

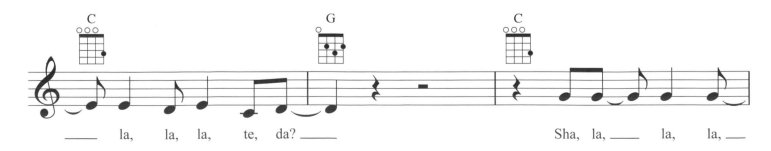

____ la, la, la, te, da? ____ Sha, la, ____ la, la,

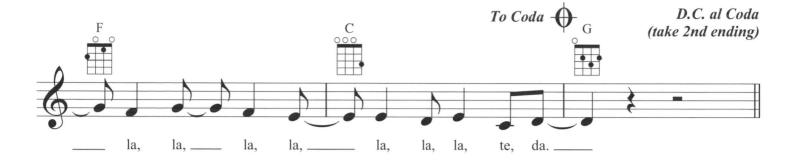

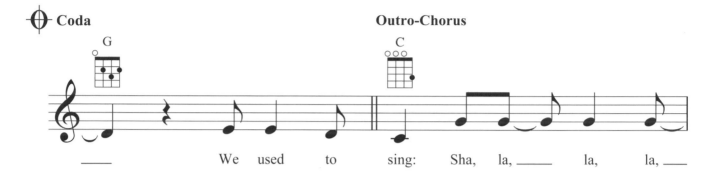

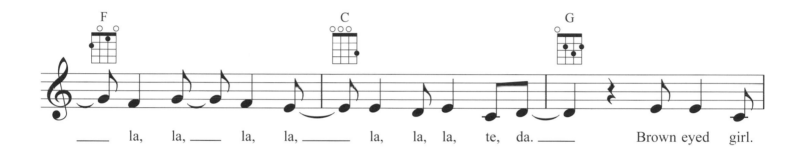

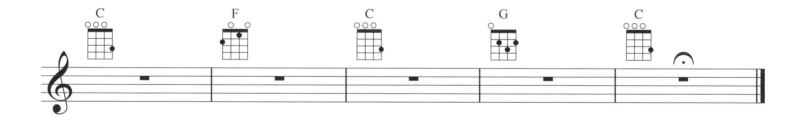

Additional Lyrics

2. Whatever happened
   To Tuesday and so slow?
   Going down the old mine
   With a transistor radio.
   Standing in the sunlight laughing,
   Hiding behind a rainbow's wall,
   Slipping and sliding
   All along the waterfall with you,
   My brown eyed girl.
   You, my brown eyed girl.

3. So hard to find my way
   Now that I'm all on my own.
   I saw you just the other day;
   My, how you have grown.
   Cast my mem'ry back there, Lord.
   Sometimes I'm overcome thinking 'bout it.
   Laughing and a-running, hey, hey,
   Behind the stadium with you,
   My brown eyed girl.
   You, my brown eyed girl.

Cruise

**Words and Music by Chase Rice, Tyler Hubbard, Brian Kelley,
Joey Moi and Jesse Rice**

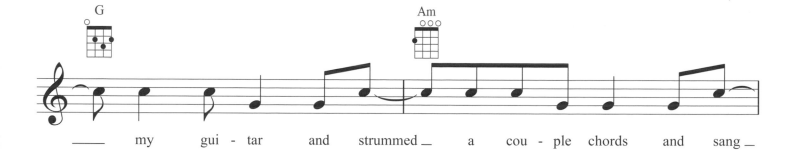

_____ my gui - tar and strummed _____ a cou - ple chords and sang _____

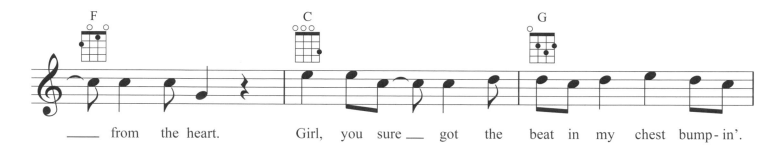

_____ from the heart. Girl, you sure _____ got the beat in my chest bump - in'.

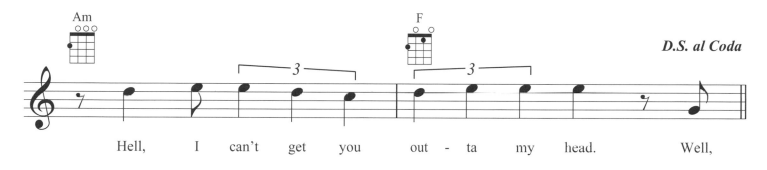

D.S. al Coda

Hell, I can't get you out - ta my head. Well,

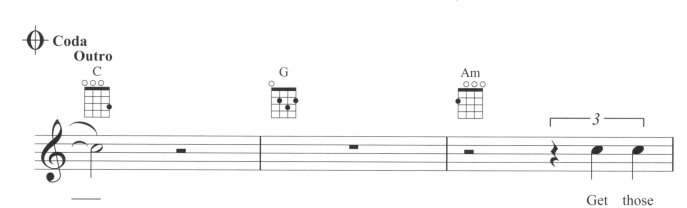

Coda
Outro

_____ Get those

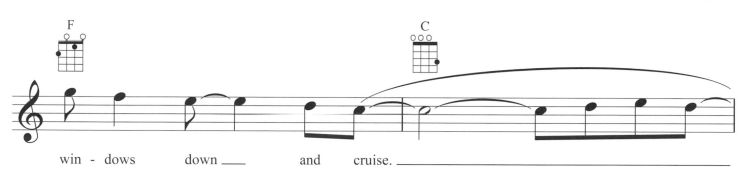

win - dows down _____ and cruise. _____

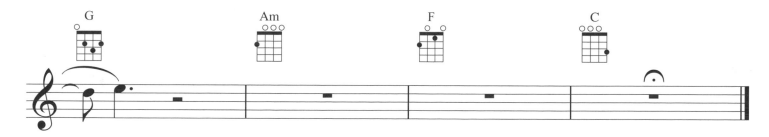

_____

Cupid

Words and Music by Sam Cooke

Verse

1. Now, ___ I don't mean to both-er you, but
2. Now, ___ Cu-pid, if your ar-row'll make her

I'm in dis-tress; ___ there's dan-ger of me los-ing all of
love strong for me, ___ I prom-ise I will love her un-til

my hap-pi-ness. ___ For I love a girl who does-n't
e-ter-ni-ty. ___ I know, be-tween the two of us, her

2nd time, D.C. al Coda

know I ex-ist, ___ and this you can fix. So,
heart we can steal; ___ help me if you will. So,

Coda

Now, ___ Cu-pid, don't you

Outro

Repeat and fade

hear me call-ing you? I need ___ you.

17

Do Wah Diddy Diddy

Words and Music by Jeff Barry and Ellie Greenwich

First note

Verse
Moderately

1. There she was, ___ just a - walk - in' down the street, sing - in',
(2.) fore I knew ___ it, she was walk - in' next to me, sing - in',

"Do wah did - dy did - dy, dum did - dy do."
"Do wah did - dy did - dy, dum did - dy do."

Snap - pin' her fin - gers and a - shuf - fl - in' her feet, sing - in',
Hold - in' my hand _____ just as nat - 'ral as can be, sing - in',

"Do wah did - dy did - dy, dum did - dy do." She looked
"Do wah did - dy did - dy, dum did - dy do." We walked

good (looked good), she looked fine (looked fine). She looked
on (walked on), to my door (my door). We walked

good, she looked fine, and I near-ly lost my mind. 2. Be -
on to my door, and then we

kissed a lit - tle more.

Whoa, _____ I knew we were fall-in' in love. ____

Yes, I did, and so I

told her all the things I'd been dream - in' _____ of. _____ Now

we're to - geth - er near - ly ev - 'ry sin - gle day, sing - in',

"Do wah did - dy did - dy, dum did - dy do."

We're so hap - py and that's how we're gon - na stay, sing - in',

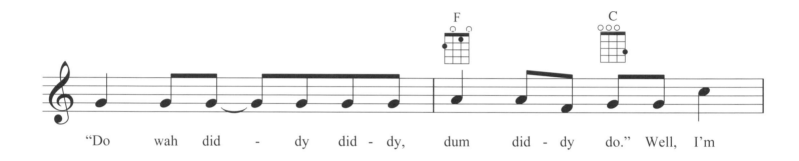

"Do wah did - dy did - dy, dum did - dy do." Well, I'm

hers (I'm hers), she's mine (she's mine). I'm

hers, she's mine; wed - ding bells are gon - na chime.

Repeat and fade

Do wah did - dy did - dy, dum did - dy do.

Greenback Dollar

Words and Music by Hoyt Axton and Ken Ramsey

First note

Verse
Moderately, with a steady beat

1. Some peo-ple say I'm a no-'count;
2. When I was a lit-tle babe,
3. Now that I'm a grown man, I've

oth-ers say I'm no good. But
my ma-ma said, "Hey, son,
trav-eled here and there. I've

I'm just a nat-'ral born trav-el-in' man
trav-el where you will and grow to be a man, and
learned that a bot-tle of bran-dy and a song, the

Chorus

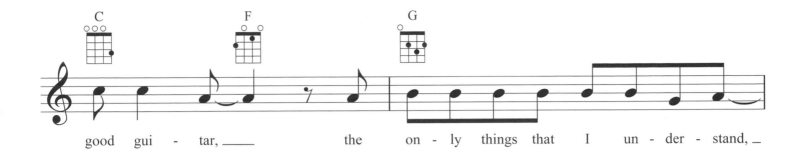

good gui - tar, _____ the on - ly things that I un - der - stand, _

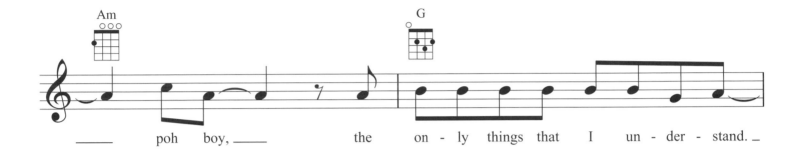

_____ poh boy, _____ the on - ly things that I un - der - stand. _

1., 2. | 3.

_____ _____ The

Outro

on - ly things that I un - der - stand, _____ poh boy, _____ the

on - ly things that I un - der - stand. _____

Duke of Earl

Words and Music by Earl Edwards, Eugene Dixon and Bernice Williams

Chorus

hurt you. Yes, I'm _____ gon - na

love you. _____ Let me hold you, _____

1.
'cause I'm the Duke of Earl. _____ 2. Yeah, _

2.
Earl. _____

Outro

Repeat and fade

Additional Lyrics

2. Yeah, and when I hold you,
   You will be my Duchess, Duchess of Earl.
   We'll walk through my dukedom,
   And the paradise we will share.

Eve of Destruction

Words and Music by P.F. Sloan and Steve Barri

Chorus

tell me o - ver and o - ver and o - ver a - gain, __ my friend, __

____ ah, you don't be - lieve we're on the eve ____ of de -

1.

struc - tion. _____

2.

struc - tion. _____

Verse

3. Yeah, my blood's so mad, feels like co - ag - u - lat - in';
   4. See additional lyrics

I'm sit - tin' here just con - tem - plat - in'. You can't twist the truth; it

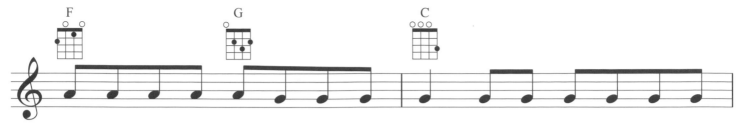

knows no reg - u - lat - in', and a hand - ful of sen - a - tors don't

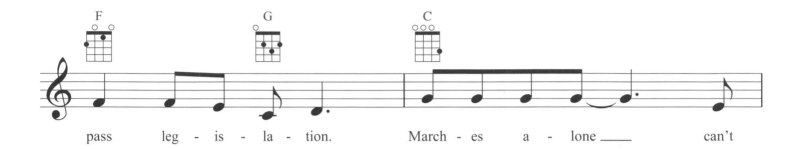

pass leg - is - la - tion. March - es a - lone ____ can't

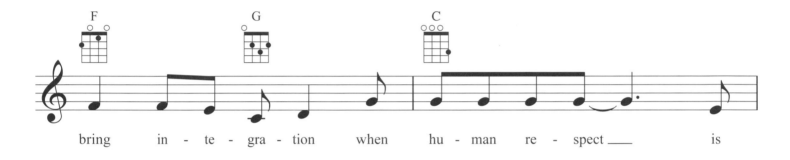

bring in - te - gra - tion when hu - man re - spect ____ is

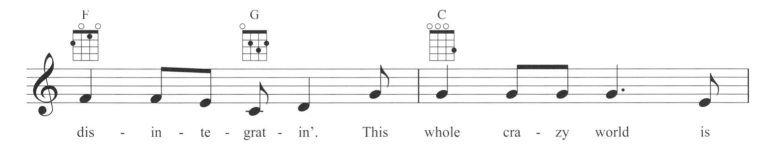

dis - in - te - grat - in'. This whole cra - zy world is

Chorus

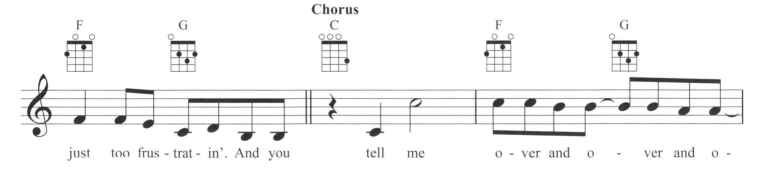

just too frus - trat - in'. And you tell me o - ver and o - ver and o -

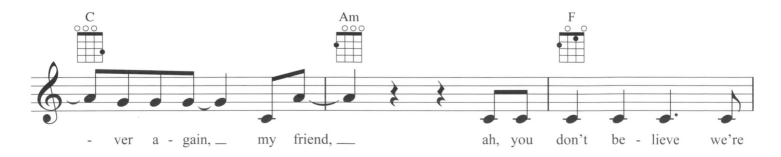

- ver a - gain, ____ my friend, ____ ah, you don't be - lieve we're

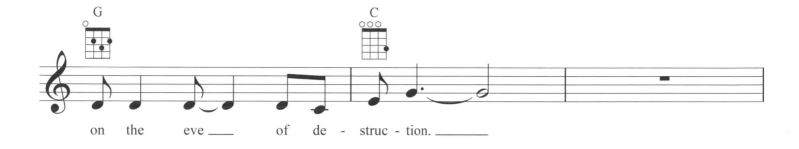

on the eve ____ of de - struc - tion. _____

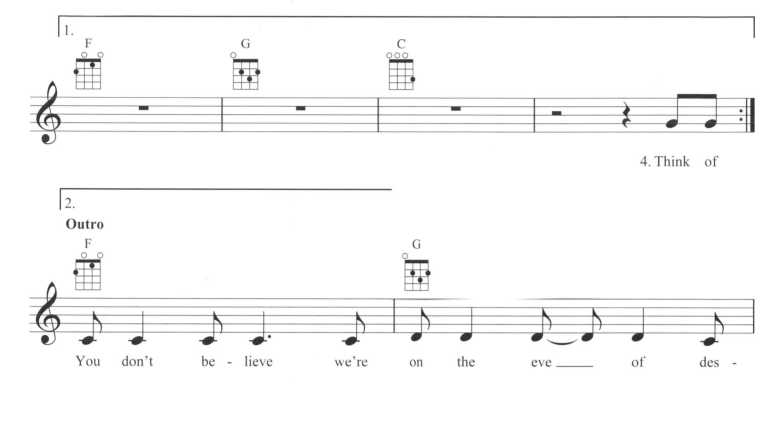

1.

4. Think of

2.

Outro

You don't be - lieve we're on the eve ____ of des -

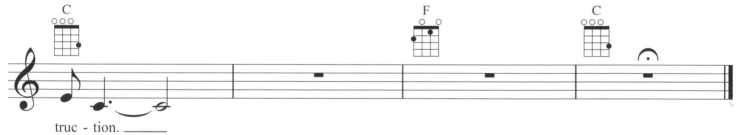

truc - tion. _____

Additional Lyrics

2. Don't you understand what I'm tryin' to say?
   Can't you feel the fears that I'm feelin' today?
   If the button is pushed, there's no runnin' away.
   There'll be no one to save with the world in a grave.
   Take a look around you, boy; it's bound to scare you, boy.

4. Think of all the hate there is in Red China,
   Then take a look around to Selma, Alabama!
   You may leave here for four days in space,
   But when you return, it's the same old place:
   The pounding drums, the pride and disgrace.
   You can bury your dead, but don't leave a trace.
   Hate your next-door neighbor, but don't forget to say grace.

Follow You Down

Words and Music by Bill Leen, Phil Rhodes, Jesse Valenzuela, Robin Wilson and D. Scott Johnson

F

fol - low ___ you down. ___

G

I'll fol - low you down, ___

To Coda ⊕

Am   F

___ but not ___ that far. ___

Bridge

G   Am   F

How you gon - na ev - er find ___ your place, ___

G   Am

run - ning an ar - ti - fi - cial pace?

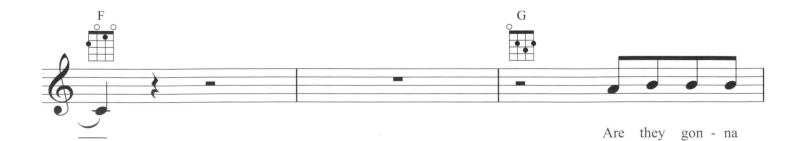

F   G

Are they gon - na

Forever & Always

Words and Music by Taylor Swift

thing is break-in' down. We al-most nev-er speak. I don't feel
com - ing down to noth-in'. Here's to si - lence that

wel - come an - y - more. __ Ba - by, what hap-pened? Please tell me, 'cause one
cuts me to the core. __ Where is this go - ing? Thought I

sec - ond it was per - fect, now you're half - way out the door. __
knew __ for a min - ute, but I don't _____ an - y - more. __

Pre-Chorus

___ } And I ___ stare at the phone. _ He still has-n't called __ and then you

feel so low you can't feel _____ noth-in' at all. __ And you flash back to _____ when he __

_____ said, "For - ev - er and al - ways." _____ Oh, _____ oh, _____ and it

% Chorus

rains in your bed - room, ev - 'ry - thing is wrong. It

rains when you're here and it rains _____ when you're gone. 'Cause

Cause

To Coda ⊕

I was there _____ when you _____ said, "For - ev - er and al - ways." _____

1. N.C.　　　　　　2.　　　　　　　　　　**Interlude**
　　　　　　　　　　　　　　　　　　　　　Am　N.C.　G　N.C.　F

2. Was I　　　You did - n't mean it, ba - by. _____

The Freshmen

Words and Music by Brian Vander Ark

1. When I was young, I knew ev - 'ry - thing.
2., 3. *See additional lyrics*

She, a punk who rare - ly ev - er took ad - vice. Now I'm

guilt - strick - en, sob - bing with my head on the floor.

Stop a ba - by's breath and a shoe - ful of rice, ___ now.

I can't be held re - spon - si - ble, ___

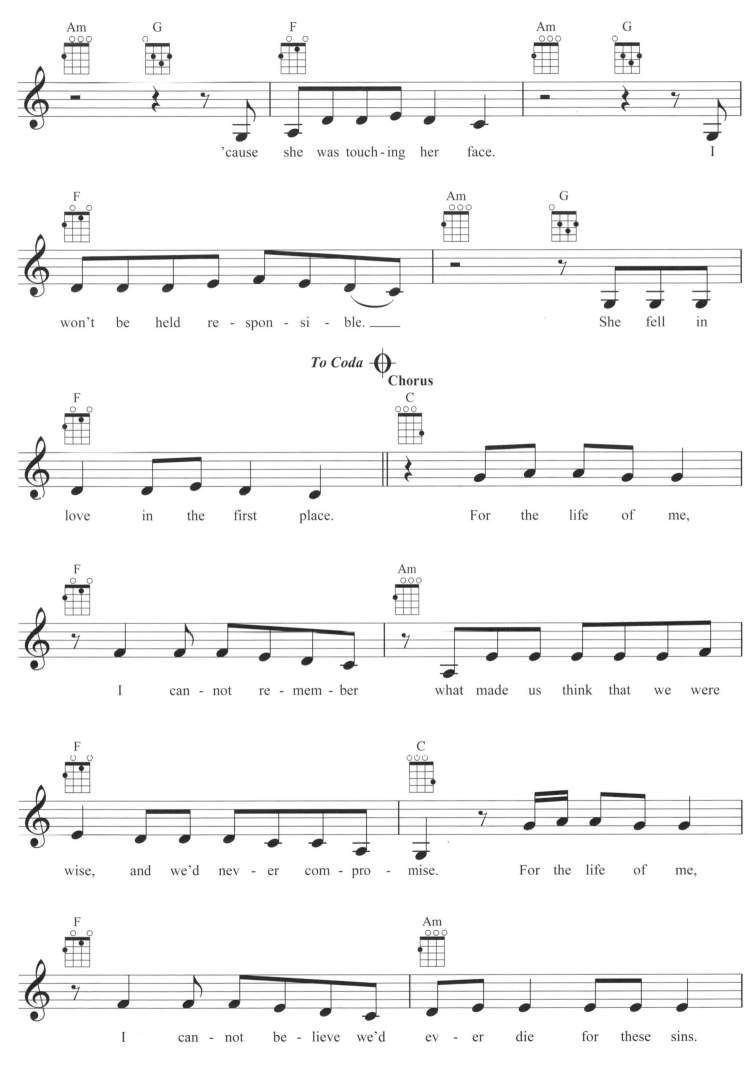

'cause she was touch-ing her face. I won't be held re-spon-si-ble. _____ She fell in

To Coda ⊕
Chorus

love in the first place. For the life of me, I can-not re-mem-ber what made us think that we were wise, and we'd nev-er com-pro-mise. For the life of me, I can-not be-lieve we'd ev-er die for these sins.

We were mere - ly fresh - men.

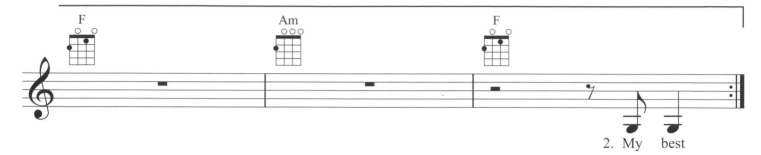

2. My best

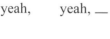
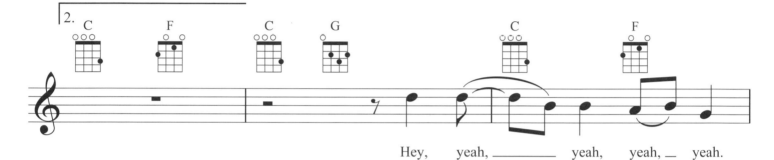

Hey, yeah, yeah, yeah, yeah.

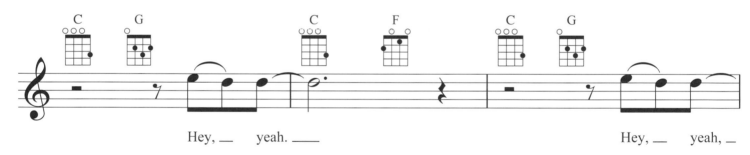

Hey, yeah. Hey, yeah,

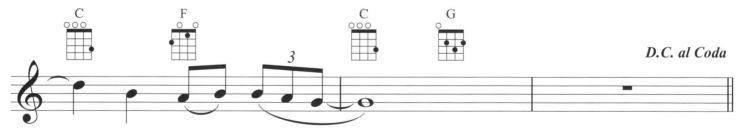

D.C. al Coda

yeah, yeah, yeah.

Coda
Chorus

For the life of me, I can - not re - mem - ber

40

Additional Lyrics

2. My best friend took a week's vacation to forget her.
   His girl took a week's worth of Valium and slept.
   And now he's guilt-stricken, sobbing with his head on the floor.
   Thinks about her now and how he never really wept. He says:

3. We tried to wash our hands of all of this.
   We never talk of a lack in relationships
   And how we're guilt-stricken, sobbing with our heads on the floor.
   We fell through the ice when we tried not to slip. We'd say:

Good Riddance
(Time of Your Life)
Words by Billie Joe
Music by Green Day

1. An - oth - er turn - ing point, ___ a fork ___
2. So take the pho - to - graphs ___ and still -

___ stuck in ___ the ___ road.   Time grabs you by ___
- frames in ___ your ___ mind.   Hang it on ___

___ the wrist, ___ di - rects ___ you where ___ to ___ go.
___ a shelf ___ in good ___ health and ___ good ___ time.

So make the best ___ of ___ this test ___ and don't ___ ask why.
Tat - toos of mem - o - ries and dead ___ skin ___ on trial. ___

___   It's not a ques - tion, but ___ a les -
___   For what it's worth, ___ it ___ was worth

Hey Ya!

Words and Music by Andre Benjamin

thought a - lone ___ is kill - ing me right now. _____

_____ Uhh. Thank God for mom and dad ___ for stick - ing

two to - geth - er 'cause we don't know how. _____

Chorus

_____ Uhh. Hey _____ ya! _____

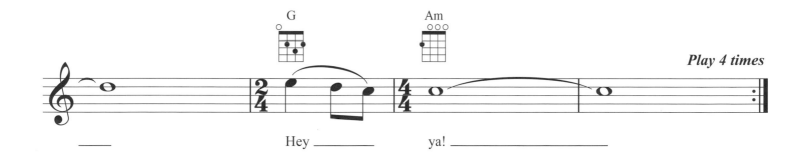

Play 4 times

_____ Hey _____ ya! _____

Verse

2. You think you've got it. Oh, _____ you think you've got it. But

got it just don't get it till there's noth - ing at all. _____

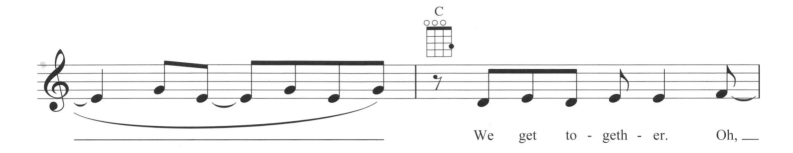

_____ We get to - geth - er. Oh, ___

___ we get to - geth - er. But sep - 'rate's al - ways bet - ter when there's

feel - ings in - volved. _____

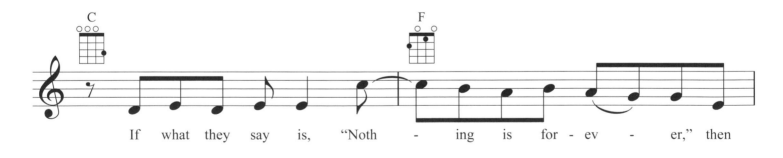

If what they say is, "Noth - ing is for - ev - er," then

what makes, then what makes, then what makes, then

what makes, then what makes, huh, love the ex - cep - tion? ___

___ So why, oh why, oh why, ___ oh why, oh why, oh, are

we so in de - ni - al when we know we're not hap - py here? ___

Chorus

___ Hey ___ ya! ___

(Spoken:) Y'all don't wanna hear me, you just wanna dance.

Hey ___ ya! ___ Don't want to meet your

dad - dy, oh, oh. ___ Just want you in my Cad - dy, oh, oh.

Oh, oh, _____ don't want to meet your

ma - ma, oh, oh. _____ Just want to make you cum-ma, oh, oh.

I'm, I'm, oh, oh, I'm just be - ing

hon - est. Oh, oh, _____ I'm just be - ing hon - est.

Outro-Chorus

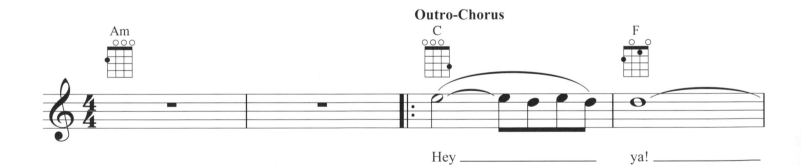

Hey _____ ya! _____

Repeat and fade

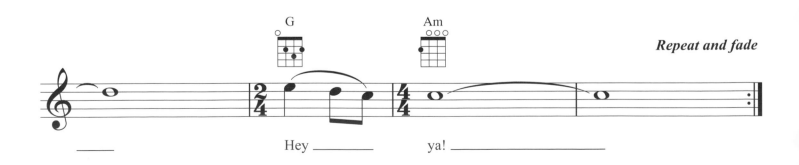

_____ Hey _____ ya! _____

Here Without You

Words and Music by Matt Roberts, Brad Arnold, Christopher Henderson and Robert Harrell

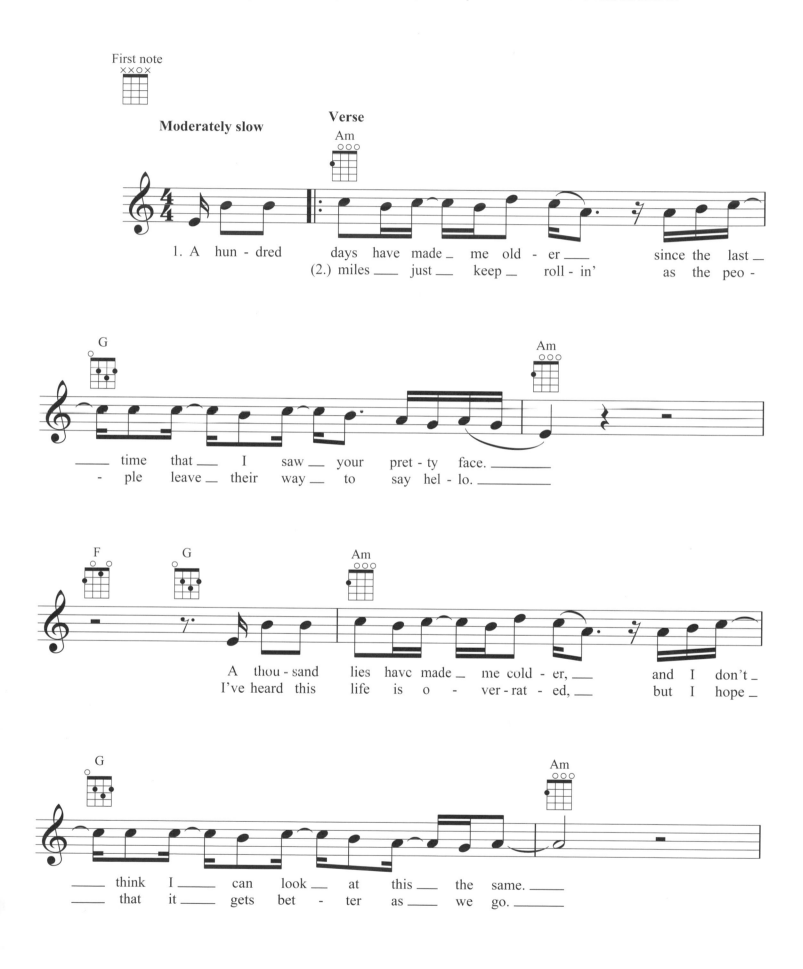

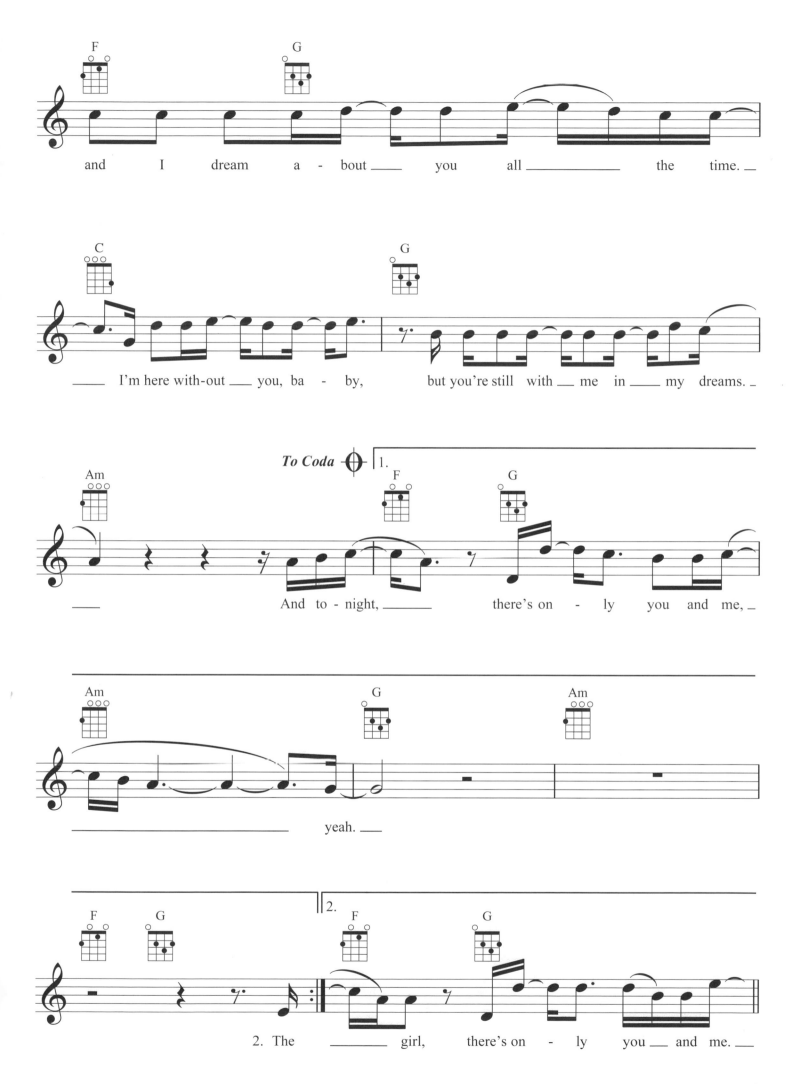

and I dream a - bout _____ you all _____ the time. _____

_____ I'm here with-out _____ you, ba - by, but you're still with _____ me in _____ my dreams. _____

To Coda 1.
_____ And to - night, _____ there's on - ly you and me, _____

_____ yeah. _____

2. The _____ girl, there's on - ly you _____ and me. _____

Bridge

Am   C

Ev - 'ry - thing ___ I know   and ev - 'ry - where ___ I   go, ___

G

it gets hard, _____ but it _____ won't take ___

F

___ a - way ___ my   love. _____

Am   C

And when the last ___ one falls,   when it's all ___ said   and done, ___

G   F

___ it gets hard, ___ but it ___ won't take _____   a - way ___   my love. ___

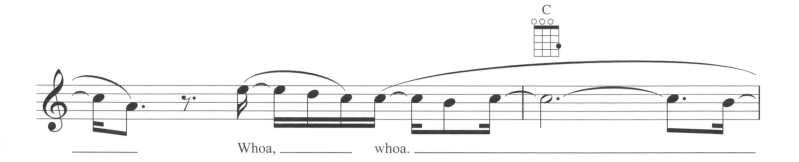

Whoa, whoa.

D.S. al Coda

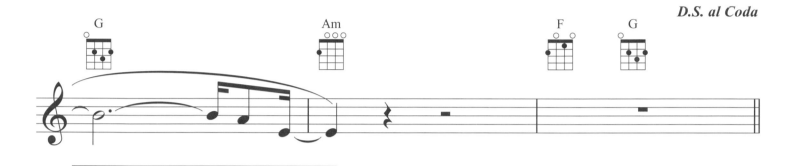

$\oplus$ **Coda**

girl, there's on - ly you ___ and me, ___

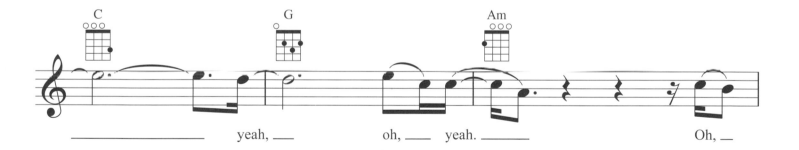

yeah, ___ oh, ___ yeah. ___ Oh, ___

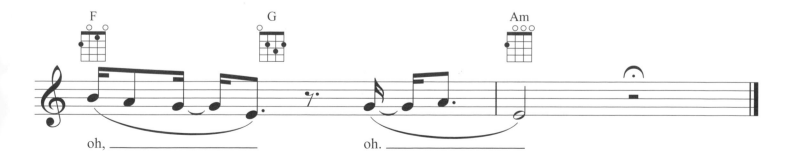

oh, ___ oh. ___

How to Save a Life

Words and Music by Joseph King and Isaac Slade

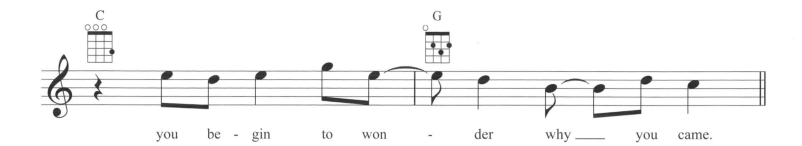

you be - gin to won - der why ____ you came.

Chorus

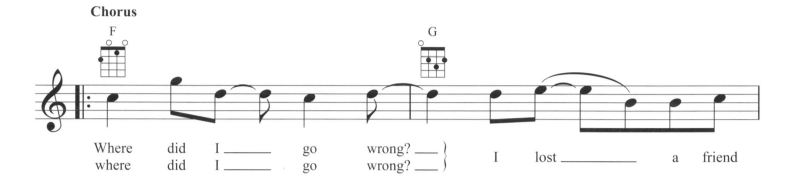

Where did I ____ go wrong? ____ } I lost _____ a friend
where did I ____ go wrong? ____ }

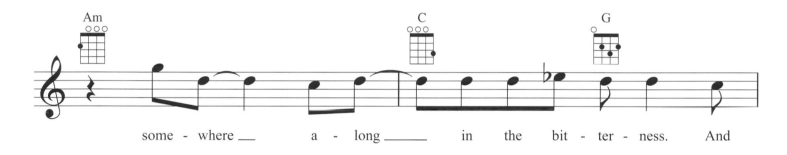

some - where ____ a - long ____ in the bit - ter - ness. And

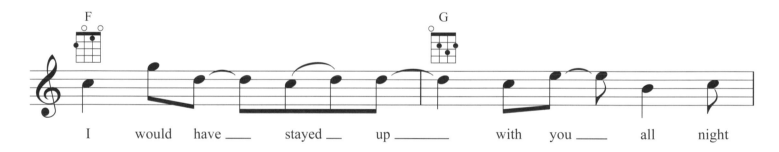

I would have ____ stayed ____ up ____ with you ____ all night

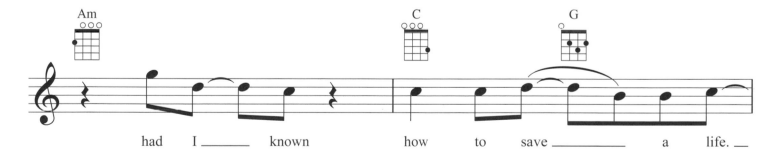

had I ____ known how to save _____ a life. ____

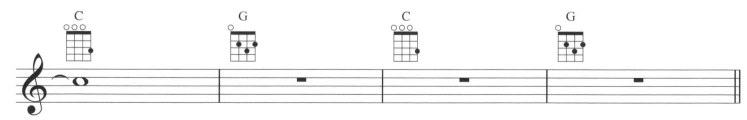

____

3. As

Verse

2. Let him know ____ that you ____ know best ____ 'cause
   he be - gins ____ to raise ____ his voice, ____ you

   af - ter all ____ you do ____ know best. ____
   low - er yours ____ and grant ____ him one ____ last choice. ____

   ____ Try to slip past his ____ de - fense ____
   ____ Drive un - til you lose ____ the road ____ or

   with - out grant - ing in - no - cence. ____
   break with the ones you've fol - lowed. ____

   Lay down ____ a list ____ of what ____ is wrong,
   He will ____ do one ____ of two ____ things: ____

   the things you've told ____ him all ____ a - long. And
   He will ad - mit to ev - 'ry - thing, ____

I Love a Rainy Night

Words and Music by Eddie Rabbitt, Even Stevens and David Malloy

I'll Be

Words and Music by Edwin McCain

Pre-Chorus

tell _____ me that we be - long ___ to -

geth - er. _____ Dress it up with the

trap - pings of ___ love. _____ I'll be ___ cap - ti -

vat - ed, I'll hang ___ from your ___ lips in -

stead of the gal - lows of heart - ache ___ that

hang from a - bove. _____

2. And

life. _____

Bridge

_____ And I've ____ dropped out, I've burned up, I've

fought my way back from the dead. _____

_____ I've

tuned in,   turned on,   re - mem - bered _____ the

thing that you   said. _____

D.S. al Coda

_____

⊕ **Coda**
Outro

life, _____

the

great - est _____ fan of your _____ life.

Ho Hey

Words and Music by Jeremy Fraites and Wesley Schultz

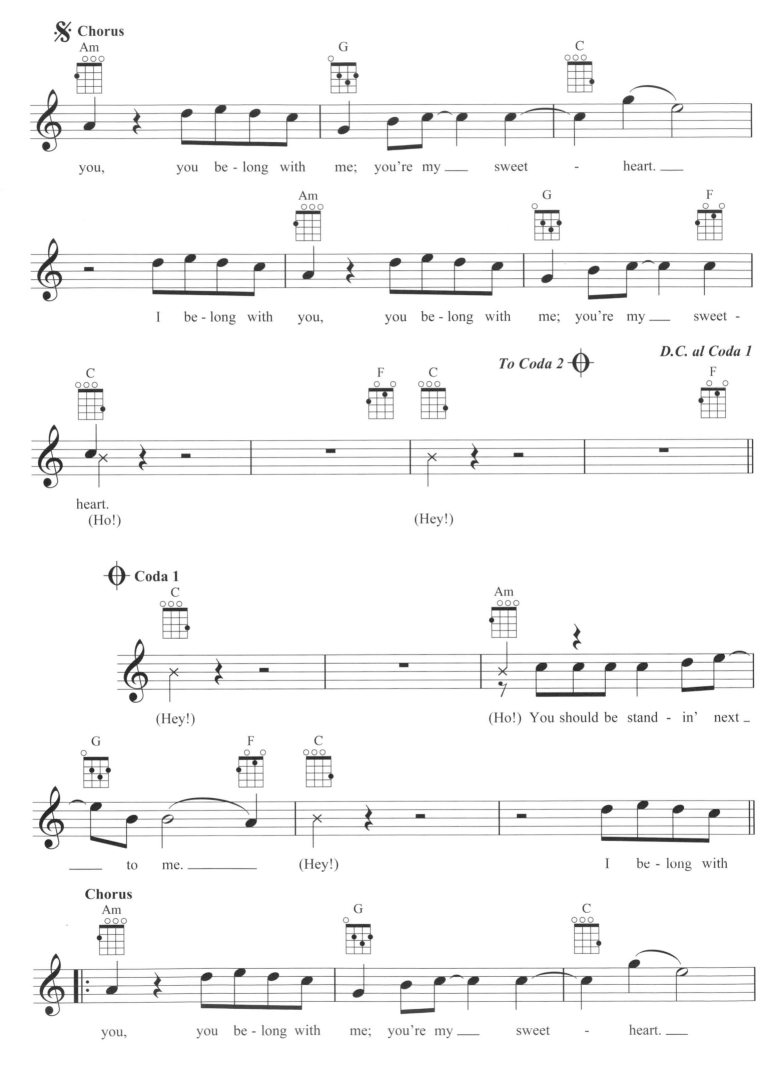

Additional Lyrics

2. (Ho!) So show me, family,
   (Hey!) All the blood that I will bleed.
   (Ho!) I don't know where I belong,
   (Hey!) I don't know where I went wrong,
   (Ho!) But I can write a song.
   (Hey!)

3. (Ho!) I don't think you're right for him.
   (Hey!) Look at what it might have been if you
   (Ho!) Took a bus to Chinatown.
   (Hey!) I'd be standing on Canal
   (Ho!) And Bowery. *(To Coda 1)*

If I Had a Hammer
(The Hammer Song)

Words and Music by Lee Hays and Pete Seeger

Additional Lyrics

2. If I had a bell, I'd ring it in the morning,
   I'd ring it in the evening all over this land.
   I'd ring out danger, I'd ring out a warning,
   I'd ring out love between my brothers and my sisters,
   All over this land.

3. If I had a song, I'd sing it in the morning,
   I'd sing it in the evening all over this land.
   I'd sing out danger, I'd sing out a warning,
   I'd sing out love between my brothers and my sisters,
   All over this land.

4. Well, I got a hammer, and I've got a bell,
   And I've got a song to sing all over this land.
   It's the hammer of justice, it's the bell of freedom,
   It's the song about love between my brothers and my sisters,
   All over this land.

Iris

Words and Music by John Rzeznik

and I _____ don't _____ wan - na go _____ home right
I just ____ don't ____ wan - na miss _____ you to -
yeah, you ____ bleed ____ just to know _____ you're a -

1.

now.

2., 3.

2. And all ____ night.}
live.}

To Coda ⊕

Chorus

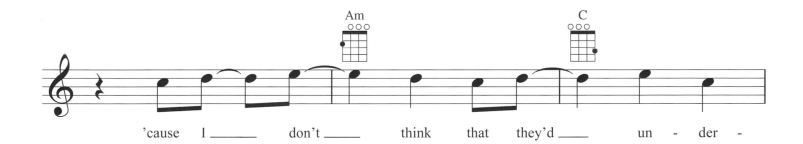

And I _____ don't want the world ____ to see me

'cause I _____ don't _____ think that they'd _____ un - der -

stand. When ev - 'ry - thing's __

made to be ___ bro - ken,   I just ___ want _

___ you to know ___ who I ___ am.

⊕ Coda
Chorus

D.S. al Coda
(take 2nd ending)

3. And you can't _   don't want the world ___ to see _

___ me   'cause I ___ don't ___ think that they'd _

___ un - der - stand.   When ev - 'ry - thing's _

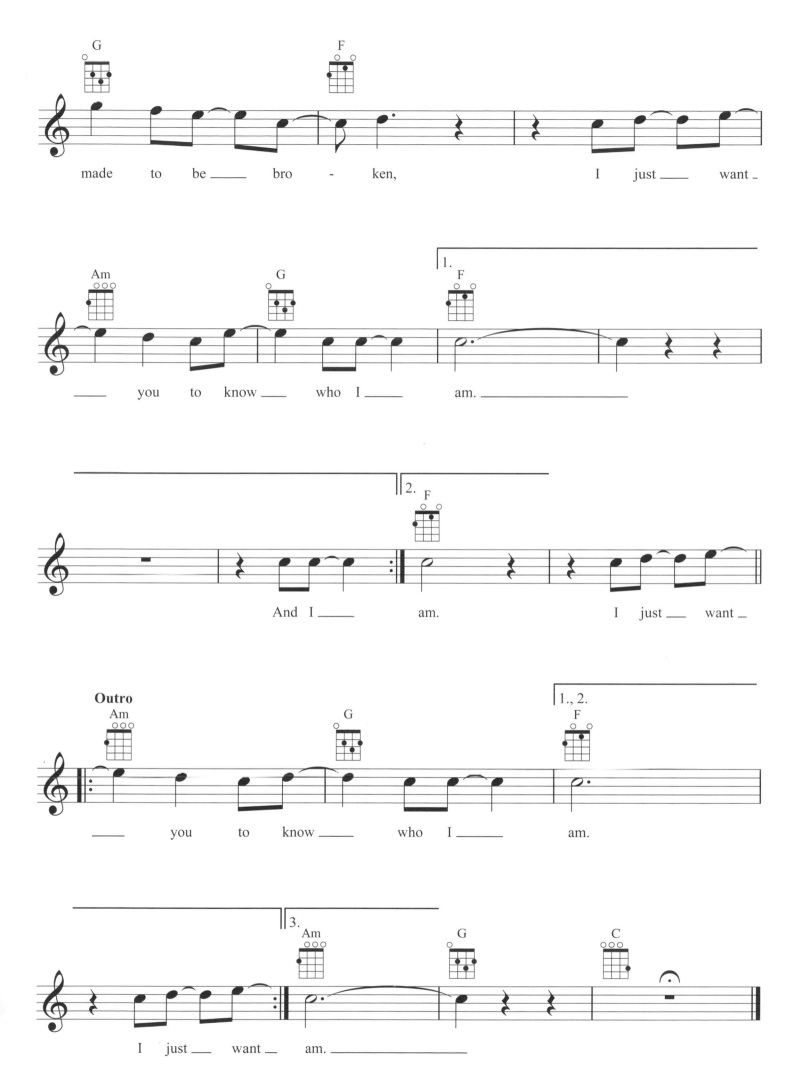

It's Only Make Believe

Words and Music by Conway Twitty and Jack Nance

First note

Intro
Freely

Peo - ple see us ev -'ry - where, __ they think you real - ly care. __

But my - self I can't de - ceive; I know it's on - ly make be -

Slowly and steadily

Verse

lieve.

1. My one and on - ly prayer
2. My hopes, my dreams come true;

is that some - day you'll care.   My hopes, my dreams come true,
my life I'd give for you,   my heart, a wed - ding ring,

my one and on - ly you.
my all, my ev - 'ry - thing.

No one will ev - er know —
My heart I can't con - trol; —

how much I love you so.
you rule my ver - y soul.

My on - ly prayer will be,

some - day you'll care for me, but it's on - ly

make - be - lieve. _____

Verse

3. My one and on - ly prayer is that some - day you'll care.

My hopes, my dreams come true, my one and on - ly you.

No one will ev - er know __ how much I love you so. _____

_____ My on - ly prayer will be, some-day you'll care for me, but it's

on - ly make _____ be -

lieve. _____

If I Had $1,000,000

Words and Music by Steven Page and Ed Robertson

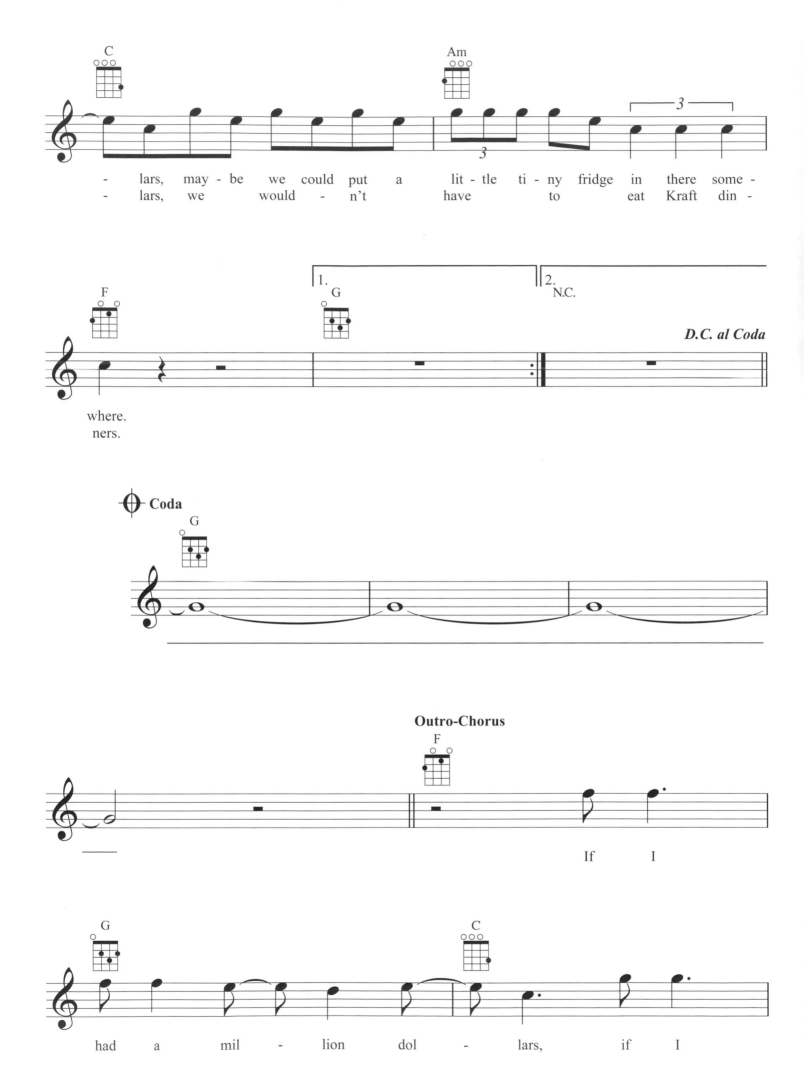

-lars, may - be we could put a lit - tle ti - ny fridge in there some -
-lars, we would - n't have to eat Kraft din -

1.
where.
2.

D.C. al Coda

ners.

Coda

Outro-Chorus

If I

had a mil - lion dol - lars, if I

80

had a mil - lion dol - lars,   if I

had a mil - lion dol - lars,   if I

had a mil - lion dol - lars,   if I

had a mil - lion dol - lars,

I'd be rich.

Jessie's Girl

Words and Music by Rick Springfield

wom-an like that? Like Jes-sie's girl, _____ I wish that I had

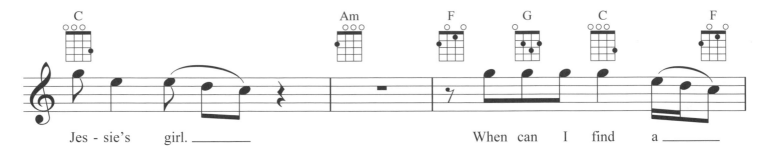

Jes - sie's girl. _____ When can I find a _____

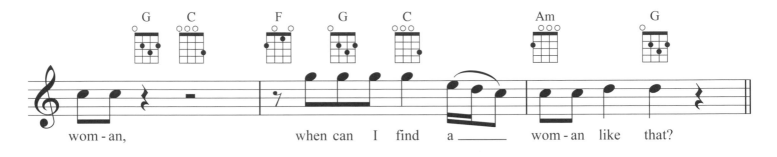

wom-an, when can I find a _____ wom-an like that?

Interlude

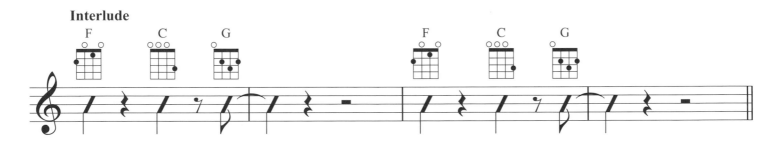

Bridge

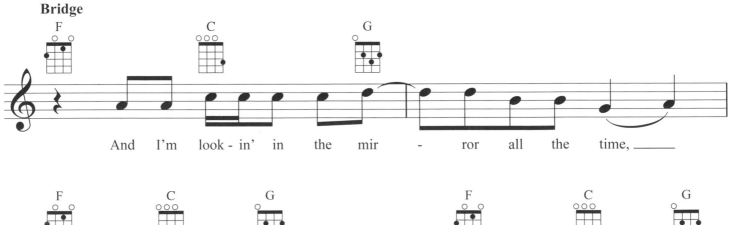

And I'm look-in' in the mir - ror all the time, _____

won - d'rin' what she don't see _____ in me. I've been fun-ny, I've been cool _____

with the lines. _____ Ain't that the way love's sup - posed _____

_____ to be? You know, I wish that I had

Outro-Chorus

Jes - sie's girl, _____ I wish that I had

Jes - sie's girl, _____ I want Jes - sie's girl. _____

1.

When can I find a _____ wom - an like that? Like

2.

rit.

85

Learning to Fly

Words and Music by Tom Petty and Jeff Lynne

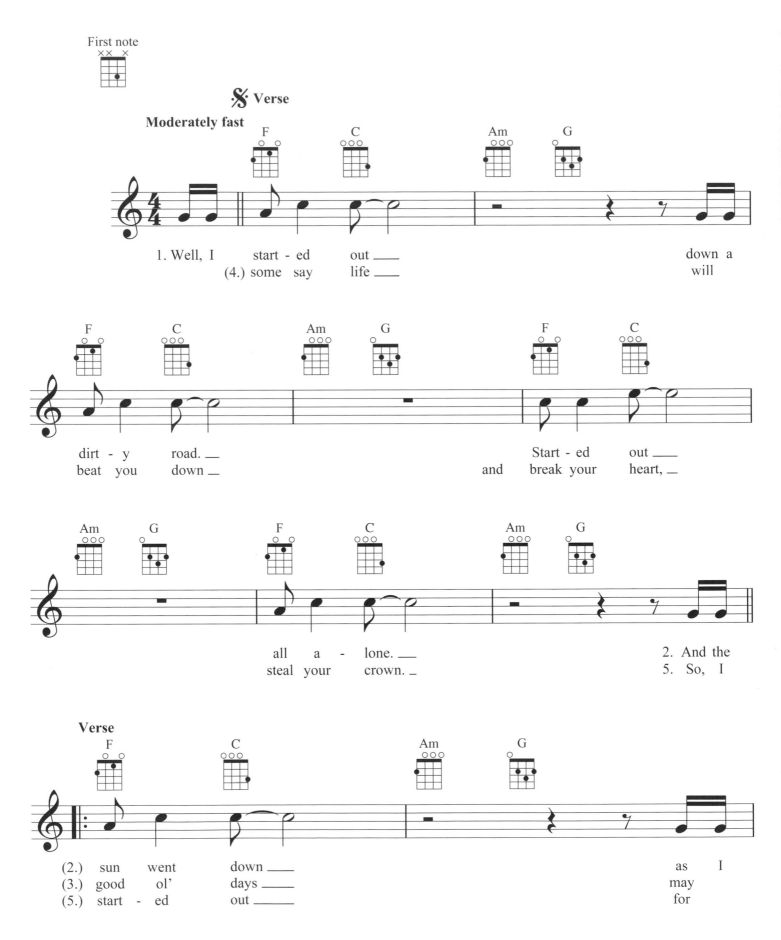

I'm learn - ing to fly ___

but I ain't got wings. ___
a - round the clouds. ___

Com - ing down ___ is the
What goes up ___

hard - est thing. ___
must come down. ___

I'm learn - ing to fly. ___

Repeat and fade

I'm

Last Kiss

Words and Music by Wayne Cochran

we had - n't driv - en   ver - y far. ___   There in the road ___
there were peo - ple stand - in' all a - round. _   Some - thing warm ___ a - run - nin'

straight a - head, ___   a car was stalled; the en - gine was dead. ___
in my eyes, ___   but I found ___ my ba - by some - how that night. __   I

I could - n't stop, ___   so I swerved to the right. ___   I'll nev - er for - get ___   the
raised her head ___ and then she smiled   and said, ___   "Hold me, dar - ling, for a

sound that night: ___ the cry - in' tires, ___   the bust - in' glass, ___   the
lit - tle while." _ I held her close, ___ I kissed her our last kiss. ___   I

pain - ful scream ___ that I heard last.   Well,
found a love ___ that I

Lookin' Out My Back Door

Words and Music by John Fogerty

First note

Verse
Moderately fast

1. Just got home from Il - li - nois, ___
(2.) gi - ant do - ing cart - wheels, a
3. For - ward trou - bles Il - li - nois, ___

lock the front ___ door, oh boy! Got to ___ sit
stat - ue wear - in' high heels. Look at all the
lock the front ___ door, oh boy! Look at all the

down, take a rest ___ on the porch. ___ I -
hap - py crea - tures danc - ing on the lawn. ___ A
hap - py crea - tures danc - ing on the lawn. ___

mag - i - na - tion sets in, pret - ty soon ___ I'm sing - in':
di - no - saur ___ Vic - tro - la lis - t'ning to ___ Buck O - wens.
Both - er me ___ to - mor - row, to - day I'll buy ___ no sor - rows.

Maps

Words and Music by Karen Orzolek, Nick Zinner and Brian Chase

One Love

Words and Music by Bob Marley

One of Us

Words and Music by Eric Bazilian

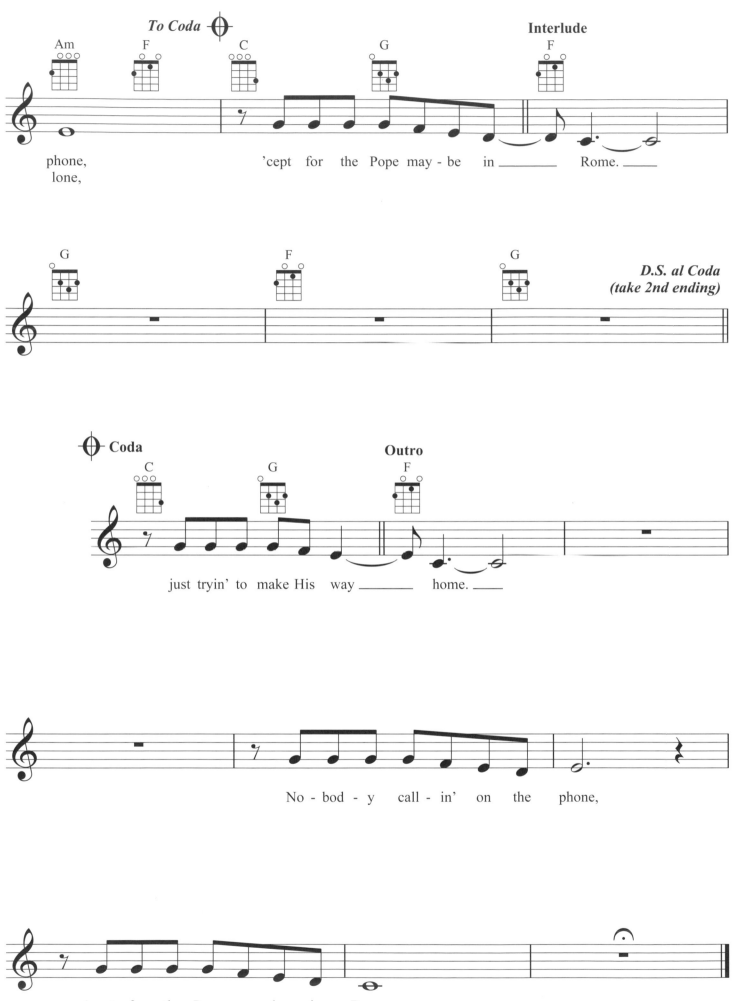

phone,
lone,
'cept for the Pope may-be in _____ Rome. _____

Interlude

D.S. al Coda
(take 2nd ending)

Coda

just tryin' to make His way _____ home. _____

Outro

No-bod-y call-in' on the phone,

'cept for the Pope may-be in Rome.

Let It Be

Words and Music by John Lennon and Paul McCartney

First note

Slowly ⅌ **Verse**

1. When I find my-self ___ in times of trou - ble,
(D.S.) *Instrumental solo*

Moth-er Mar - y comes to me, speak-ing words of wis - dom, let it

be. ___ And in my hour of dark - ness, she is

stand-ing right in front ___ of me, ___ speak-ing words of wis - dom, let it

Chorus

be. ___ }
Solo ends
Let it be, ___ let it be, ___ let it be, ___

_____ let it be. _____ Whis-per words _ of wis - dom, let it be. _

Verse

_____ 2. And when the bro - ken - heart - ed peo - ple
3. And when the night _ is cloud - y, there is

liv - ing in _____ the world a - gree, there will be an an - swer, let it
still a light _ that shines on me, shine un - til to - mor - row, let it

be. _____ For though they may be part - ed, there is
be. _____ I wake up to the sound _ of mu - sic,

still a chance that they _ will see, _ there will be an an - swer, let it
Moth - er Mar - y comes _ to me, _ speak - ing words of wis - dom, let it

Chorus

be. ———
be. ———

Let it be, ——— let it be, ——— let it be, —

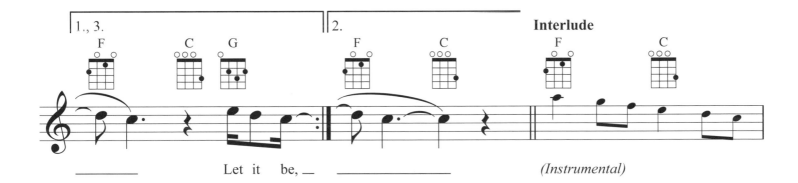

To Coda ⊕

——— let it be. —

{ 1., 3. There will be ——— an an - swer,
{ 2., 4. Whis-per words _ of wis - dom, } let it be. —

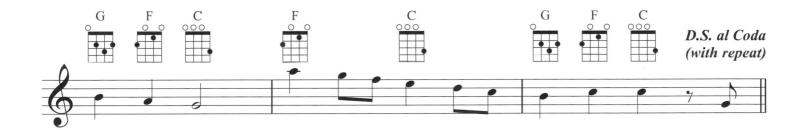

1., 3.   2. **Interlude**

———   Let it be, _ ———————   *(Instrumental)*

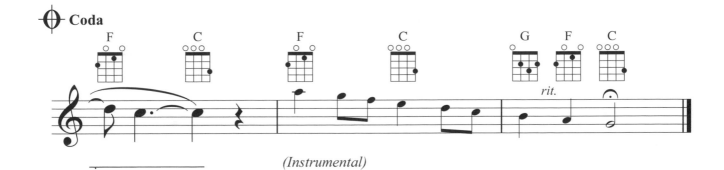

***D.S. al Coda*
*(with repeat)***

⊕ **Coda**

rit.

(Instrumental)

Please Mr. Postman

Words and Music by Robert Bateman, Georgia Dobbins,
William Garrett, Freddie Gorman and Brian Holland

('Cause it's been a might - y long time)

Post - man. Whoa, —

(since I heard from this boy - friend of mine.)

yeah. —

Verse

1. There must be some word to - day _____
2. *See additional lyrics*

from my boy - friend so ____ far a - way. ____

Please, Mis - ter Post - man, look and see. ____

Is there a let - ter, a let - ter for me?

I've been stand - ing here wait - ing, Mis - ter Post - man, _____

so, _____ so pa - tient - ly _____

for just a card or just a let - ter

say - ing he's re - turn - ing home to me. Please, Mis - ter

Additional Lyrics

2. So many days you've passed me by.
   You saw the tears standing in my eye.
   You wouldn't stop to make me feel better
   By leaving me a card or a letter.
   Please, Mr. Postman, look and see.
   Is there a letter, oh yeah, in your bag for me?
   You know it's been so long, yeah,
   Since I heard from this boyfriend of mine.

Peace Train

Words and Music by Cat Stevens

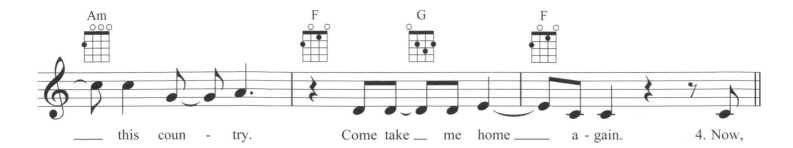

_____ this coun - try. Come take _____ me home _____ a - gain. 4. Now,

Verse

I've been _____ smil - in' late - ly, _____ think-in' a - bout _____ the good things _

6., 8. *See additional lyrics*

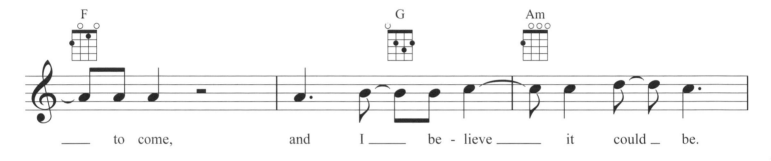

_____ to come, and I _____ be - lieve _____ it could _ be.

Chorus

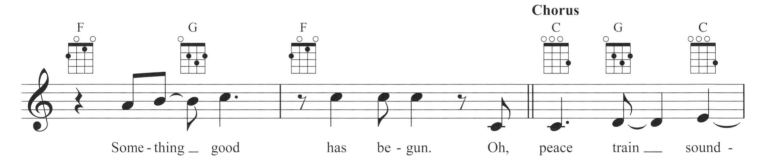

Some - thing _ good has be - gun. Oh, peace train _____ sound -

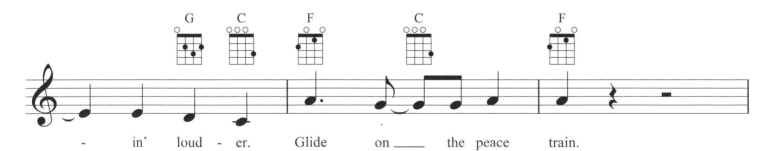

- in' loud - er. Glide on _____ the peace train.

To Coda 1 ⊕

Come on _____ the peace train.

Additional Lyrics

5. Get your bags together.
   Go bring your good friends, too.
   Because it's gettin' nearer.
   It soon will be with you.

6. Oh, come and join the living;
   It's not so far from you,
   And it's gettin' nearer.
   Soon it will all be true.

7. Now, I've been cryin' lately,
   Thinkin' about the world as it is.
   Why must we go on hating?
   Why can't we live in bliss?

8. 'Cause out on the edge of darkness,
   There rides a peace train.
   Oh, peace train, take this country.
   Come take me home again.

Roses Are Red, My Love

Words and Music by Al Byron and Paul Evans

Bridge

Then I went far a - way and you found some - one

new. I read your let - ter, dear, and I wrote back to

Chorus

you: Ros - es are red, my love, vio - lets are

blue. _____ Sug - ar is sweet, my love; good luck, may God bless

you. 3. Is that your

D.S. al Coda

Coda

you. _____

Additional Lyrics

2. We dated through high school,
   And when the big day came,
   I wrote into your book
   Next to my name:

3. Is that your little girl?
   She looks a lot like you.
   Someday some boy will write
   In her book, too:

Rude

Words and Music by Nasri Atweh, Mark Pellizzer, Alex Tanas, Ben Spivak and Adam Messinger

’cause I know that you’re an old-fash-ioned man.
you know she’s in love with me. She will go

Pre-Chorus

an-y-where I go. Can I have your daugh-ter for the rest of my life? — Say

yes, say yes, ’cause I need to know. You say I’ll nev-er get your bless-ing till the

day __ I die. __ Tough luck, my friend, { but the an-swer is no. }
{ ’cause the an-swer’s still no. }

Chorus

Why you got-ta be so rude? _____ Don’t you know I’m

hu-man, too? _____ Why you got-ta be so rude? _____

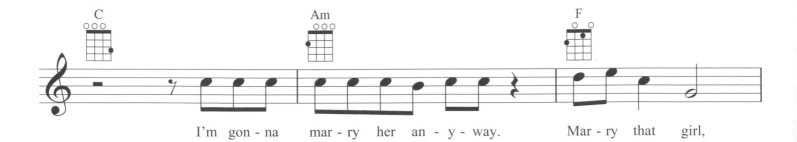

I'm gon - na   mar - ry   her   an - y - way.   Mar - ry   that   girl,

mar - ry   her   an - y - way.   Mar - ry   that   girl,   yeah,   no   mat - ter   what   you   say.

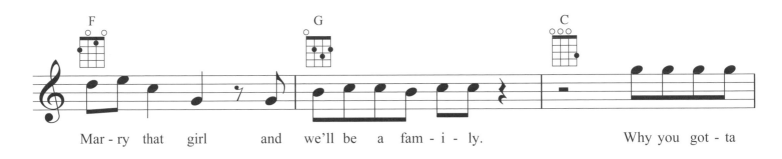

Mar - ry   that   girl   and   we'll   be   a   fam - i - ly.   Why   you   got - ta

To Coda ⊕

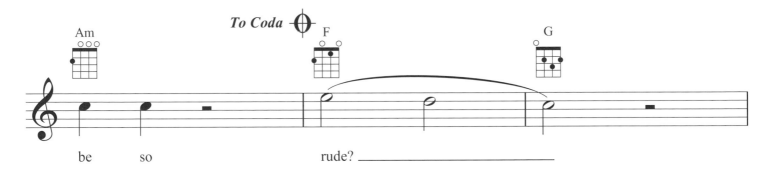

be   so   rude? _____

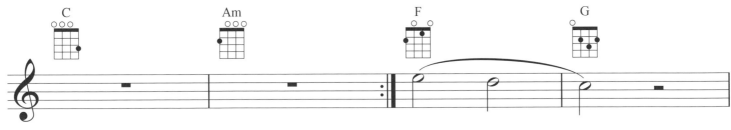

Rude. _____

Pre-Chorus

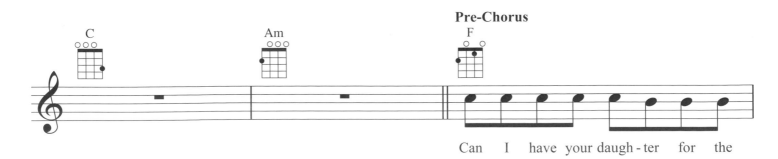

Can   I   have   your   daugh - ter   for   the

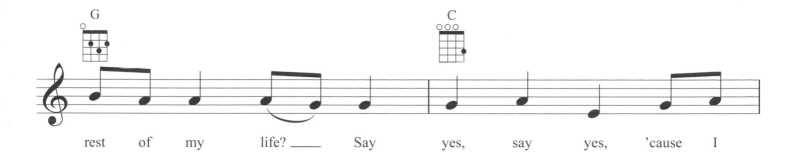

rest of my life? ____ Say yes, say yes, 'cause I

need to know. You say I'll nev - er get your bless - ing till the

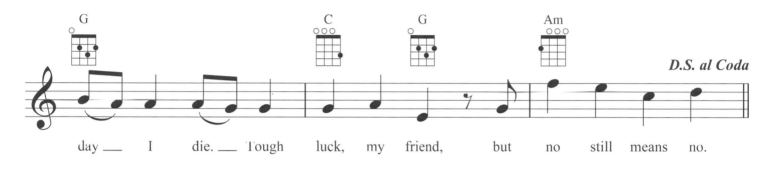

D.S. al Coda

day ___ I die. ___ Tough luck, my friend, but no still means no.

Coda

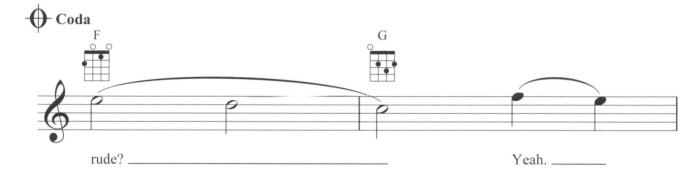

rude? _____ Yeah. _____

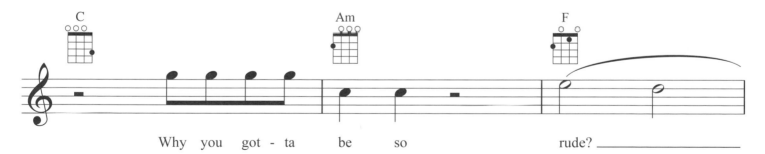

Why you got - ta be so rude? _____

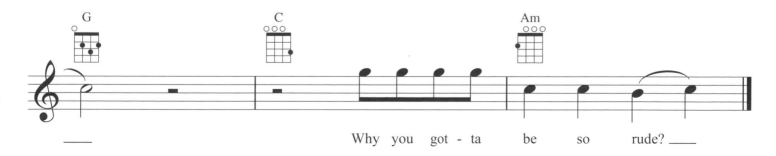

___ Why you got - ta be so rude? ___

Save Tonight

Words and Music by Eagle Eye Cherry

Chorus

Bridge

mor - row comes to take me a - way. I wish that I, that

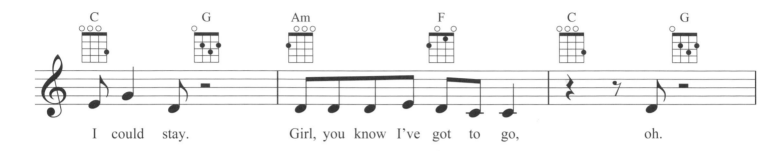

I could stay. Girl, you know I've got to go, oh.

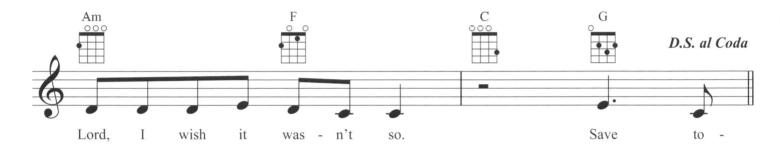

D.S. al Coda

Lord, I wish it was - n't so. Save to -

Coda

Outro

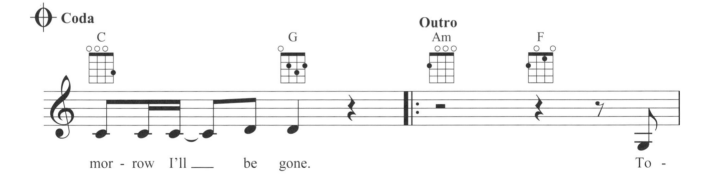

mor - row I'll ___ be gone. To -

Play 4 times

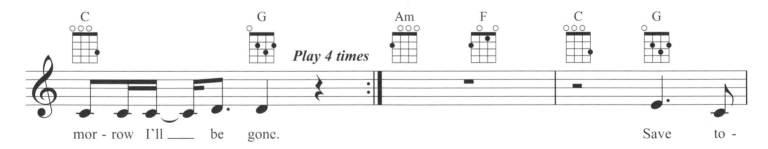

mor - row I'll ___ be gone. Save to -

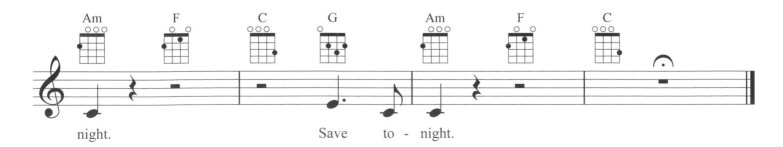

night. Save to - night.

Poker Face

Words and Music by Stefani Germanotta and RedOne

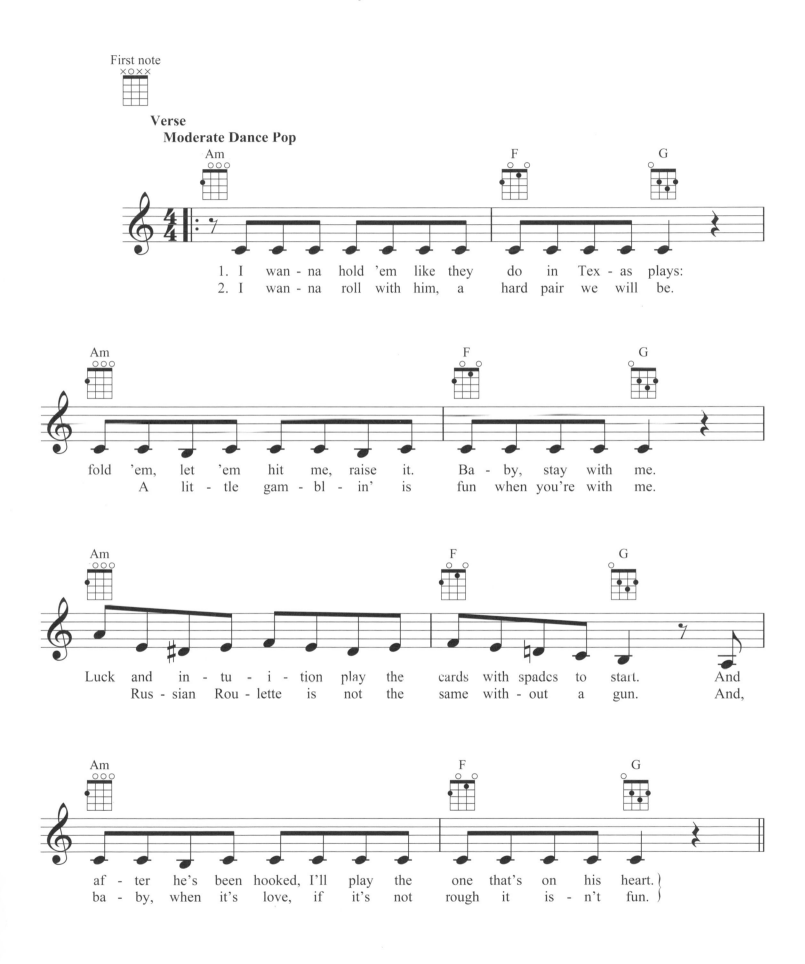

Pre-Chorus

Oh, whoa, ___ oh, oh, oh, ___ oh,

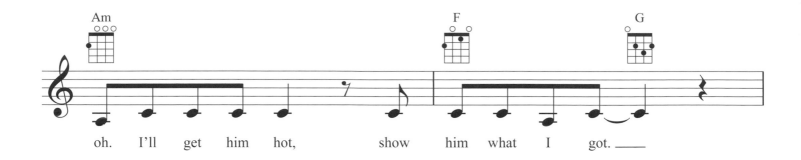

oh. I'll get him hot, show him what I got. ___

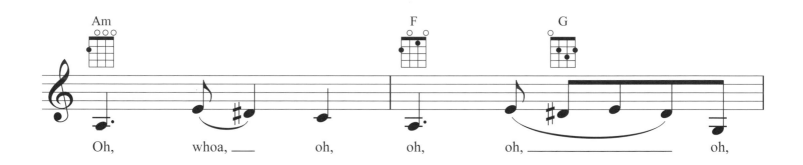

Oh, whoa, ___ oh, oh, oh, ___ oh,

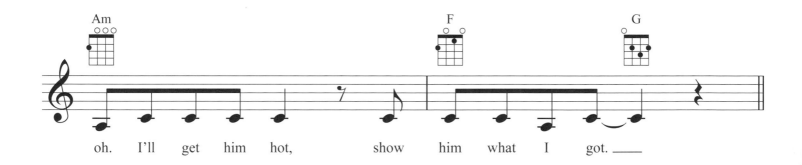

oh. I'll get him hot, show him what I got. ___

𝄋 Chorus

Can't read my, ___ can't read my, ___ no, he can't read ___ my

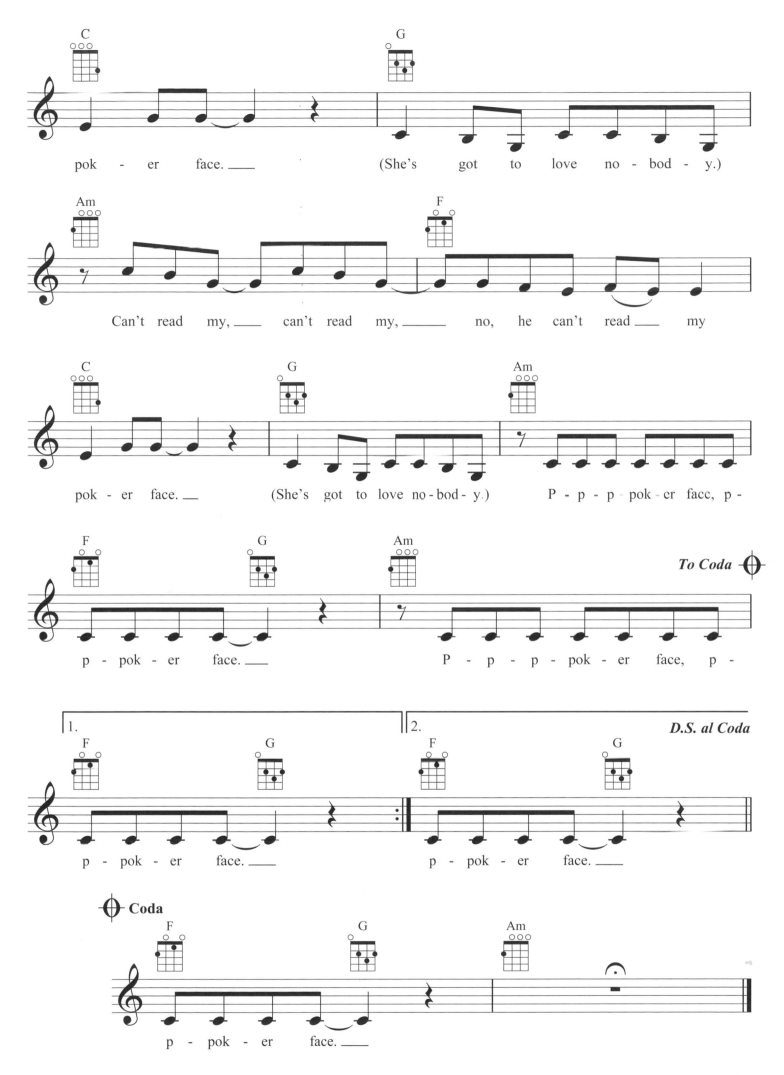

The Scientist

Words and Music by Guy Berryman, Jon Buckland, Will Champion and Chris Martin

heads on a si - lence a - part. _____

Chorus

No - bod - y said _____ it was eas - y. _____

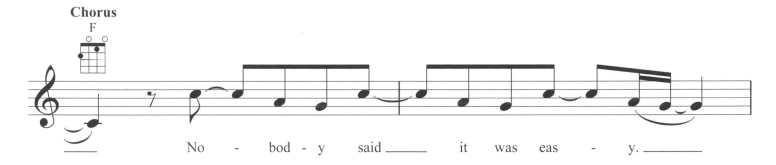

Oh, it's _____ such a shame _____ for us to part. _____

_____ No - bod - y said _____ it was eas - y. _____

_____ No _____ one ev - er { said _____ it would be this _____ hard. _____
said it would be so _____ hard. _____

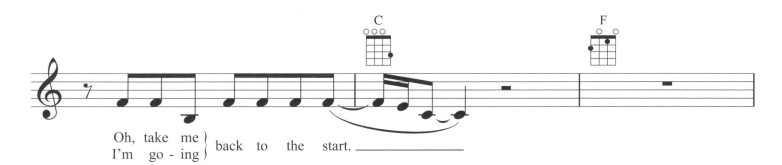

Oh, take me } back to the start. _____
I'm go - ing }

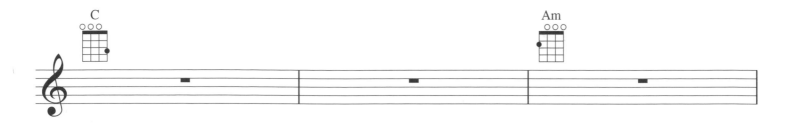

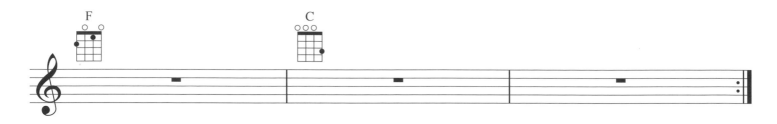

Outro

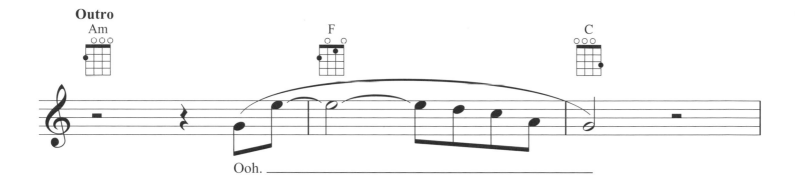

Ooh.

Ah, ooh.

Ah, ooh.

Additional Lyrics

2. I was just guessing at numbers and figures,
   Pulling the puzzles apart.
   Questions of science, science and progress
   Do not speak as loud as my heart.
   And tell me you love me, come back and haunt me.
   Oh, and I rush to the start.
   Running in circles, chasing tails,
   Coming back as we are.

Stand by Me

Words and Music by Jerry Leiber, Mike Stoller and Ben E. King

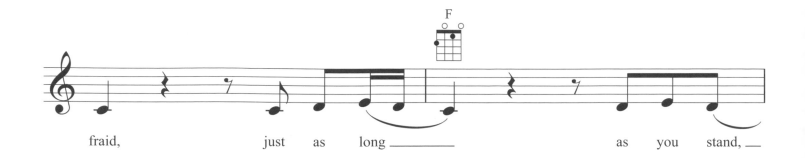

fraid,   just as   long _____   as you stand, __

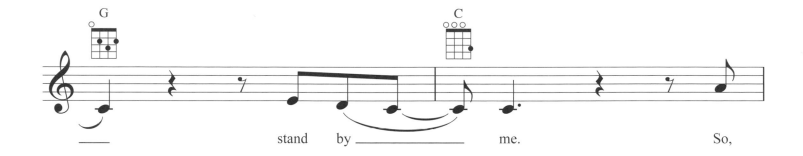

__   stand by _____ me.   So,

Chorus

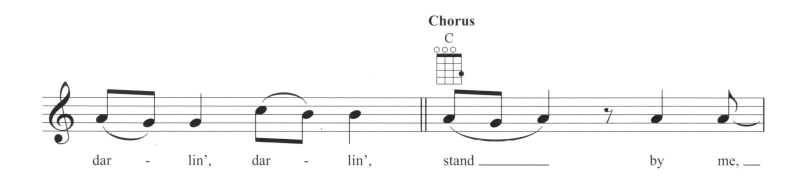

dar - lin', dar - lin', stand _____ by me, __

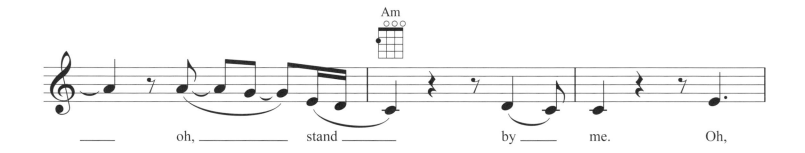

__ oh, _____ stand _____ by __ me.   Oh,

stand, __   stand by __ me,   stand by __ me.

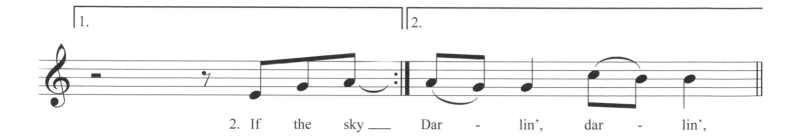

2. If the sky ___ Dar - lin', dar - lin',

Outro-Chorus

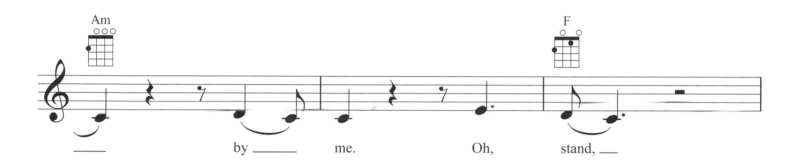

stand _____ by me, _____ oh, _____ stand ___

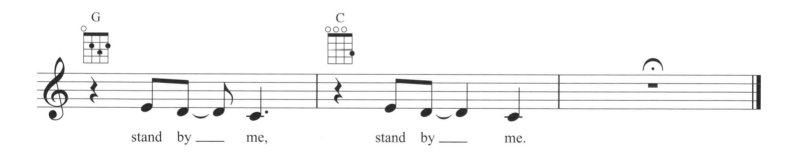

___ by ___ me. Oh, stand, ___

stand by ___ me, stand by ___ me.

Additional Lyrics

2. If the sky that we look upon should tumble and fall,
   Or the mountains should crumble to the sea,
   I won't cry, I won't cry. No, I won't shed a tear,
   Just as long as you stand, stand by me.
   And darlin', darlin'... (*To Chorus*)

Shattered
(Turn the Car Around)

Words and Music by Gregg Wattenberg and Marc Roberge

Verse
Moderate Pop Rock

1. In a way, __ I need a change __ from this burn - out scene: __

__ an - oth - er time, __ an - oth - er town, ___ an - oth - er ev - 'ry - thing. __

__ But it's al - ways back __ to you. ___

Verse

Stum - ble out _____ in the night __
2. I had no i - dea _____ that the night __

__ from the pour - ing rain. __ Made the block, __ sat and thought __
__ would take so __ damn long. __ Took it out __ on the street __

there's more I need. _____   It's al - ways back _ to you. _____
while the rain still falls.   Push me back _ to you. _____

Pre-Chorus

_____   Well, / But } I'm good _____ with - out _

_____ ya,   yeah, I'm good _____ with - out _____ you.   Yeah, _____

Chorus

_____ yeah, _____ yeah. _____   (1.,2.) How man - y times _ can I break _
(D.S.) All that I feel _ is the real -

_____ 'til I shat - ter?   O - ver the line _ can't de - fine _ what I'm af - ter. I
- ness I'm fak - in'.   Tak - in' my time, _ but it's time _ that I'm wast - in'.

al - ways — turn the car — a - round. Give me a break; — let me make —
Al - ways — turn the car — a - round. How man - y times — can I break —

— my own pat - tern. All that it takes — is some time, — but I'm shat - tered. I
— 'til I shat - ter? O - ver the line — can't de - fine — what I'm af - ter. I

To Coda

al - ways — turn the car — a - round.
al - ways — turn the car — a - round.

Bridge

Give it up, give it up, ba - by.

Give it up, give it up now, — now. —

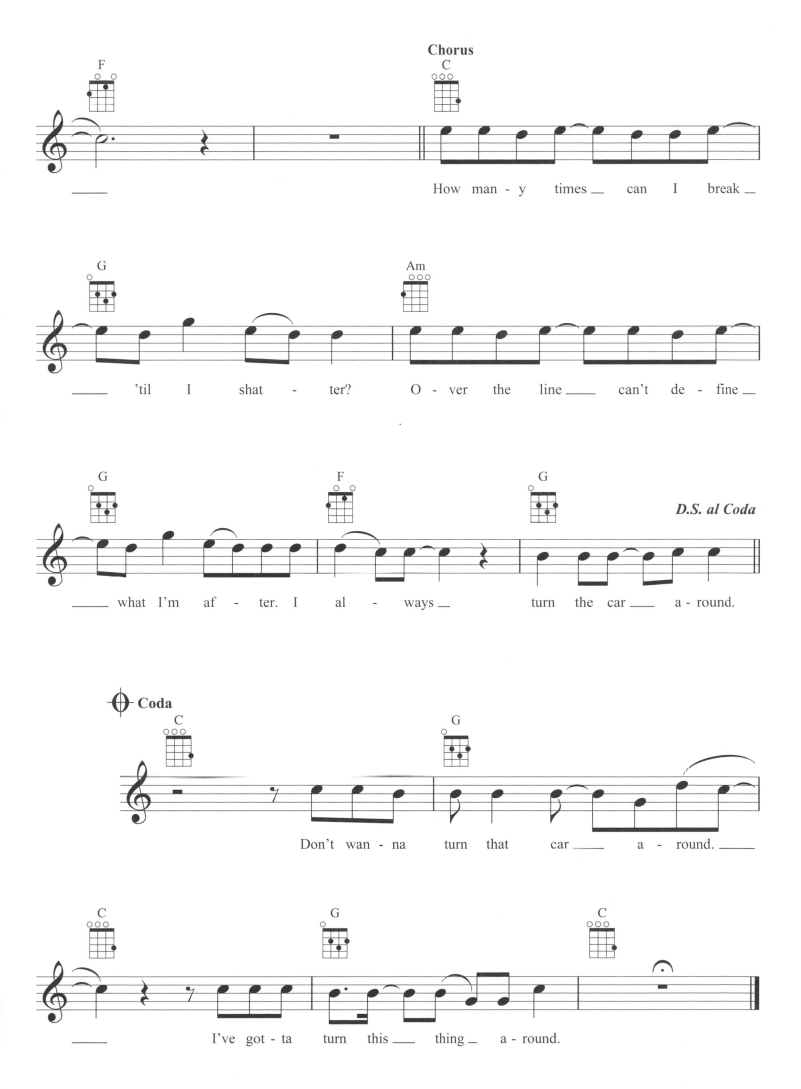

Teardrops on My Guitar

Words and Music by Taylor Swift and Liz Rose

Pre-Chorus

Chorus

Talk

Words and Music by Guy Berryman, Jon Buckland, Will Champion, Chris Martin, Ralf Huetter, Emil Schult and Karl Bartos

First note

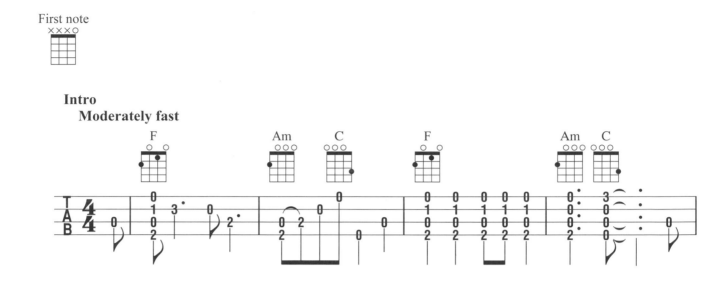

Intro
Moderately fast

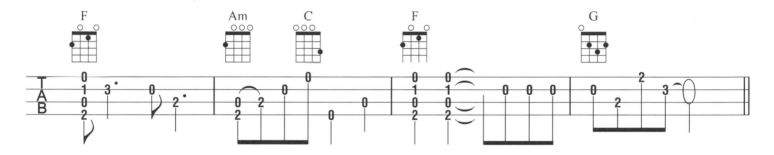

Verse

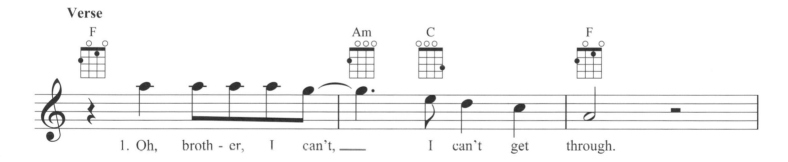

1. Oh, broth-er, I can't, ___ I can't get through.

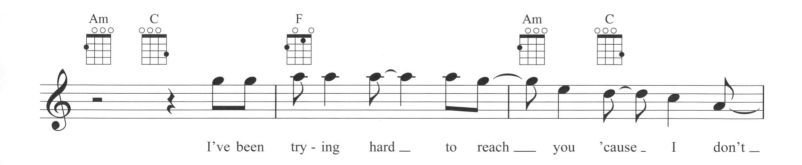

I've been try-ing hard ___ to reach ___ you 'cause ___ I don't ___

know what to do. _____ Oh, broth - er, I can't _____ be - lieve it's true. I'm so scared a - bout the fu - ture and _____ I want _____ to talk to you. _____ Oh, I want _____ to talk to you. _____

You could

𝄋 **Chorus**

(1., 2.) take a pic - ture of some - thing you see. _____
(3.) don't know where you're go - ing and you want to talk. _____

To Coda 2

To Coda 1

Verse

139

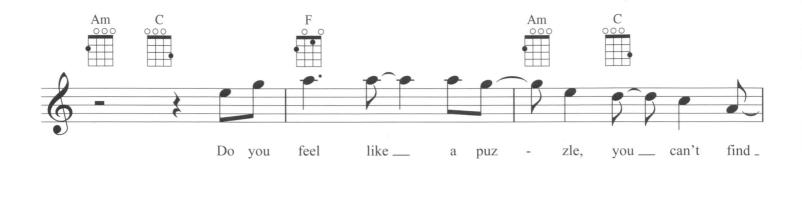

Do you feel like ___ a puz - zle, you ___ can't find ___

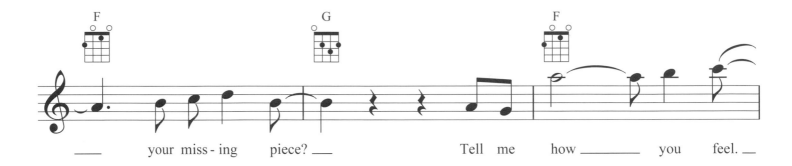

___ your miss - ing piece? ___ Tell me how _____ you feel. ___

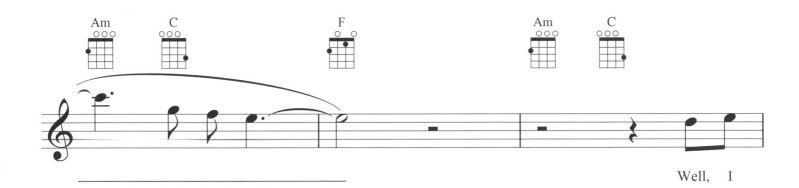

_____ Well, I

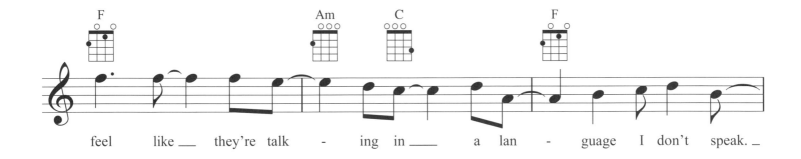

feel like ___ they're talk - ing in ___ a lan - guage I don't speak. ___

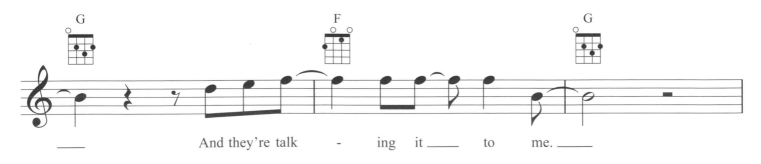

___ And they're talk - ing it ___ to me. ___

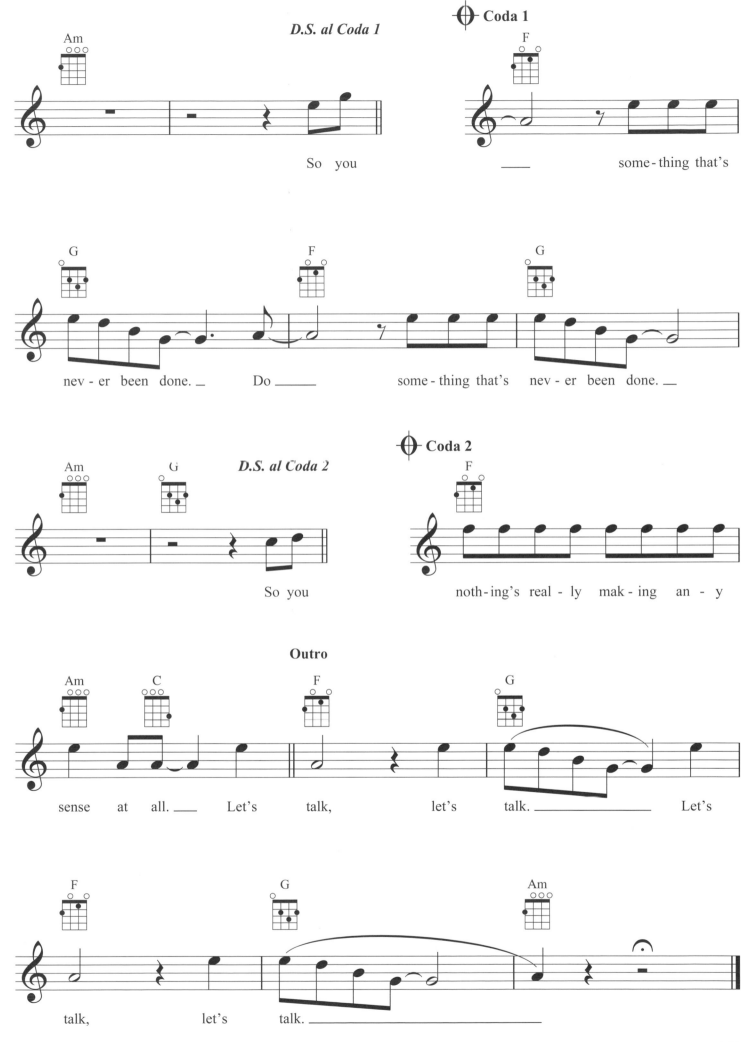

A Teenager in Love

Words by Doc Pomus
Music by Mort Shuman

Bridge

I cried a tear for no - bod - y but you.

D.C. al Coda

I'll be a lone - ly one if you should say we're through.

Coda

love, in love? _____

Additional Lyrics

2. One day I feel so happy, next day I feel so sad.
   I guess I'll learn to take the good with the bad.

3. If you want to make me cry, that won't be so hard to do.
   And if you should say goodbye, I'll still go on loving you.

Toes

Words and Music by Shawn Mullins, Zac Brown, Wyatt Durrette and John Driskell Hopkins

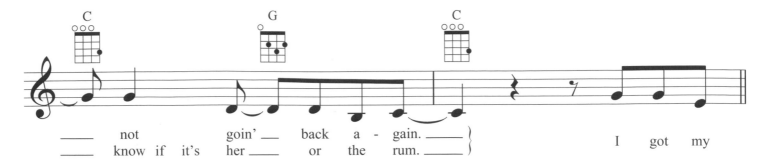

_____ not ____ goin' ___ back a - gain. _____
_____ know if it's her ___ or the rum. _____

I got my

Pre-Chorus

toes in the wa - ter, ass ____ in the sand, ___ not a wor -

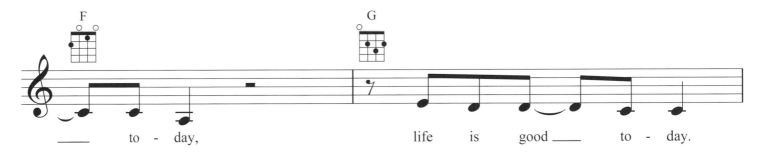

- ry in the world, ___ a cold beer in my hand. ___ Life is good ___

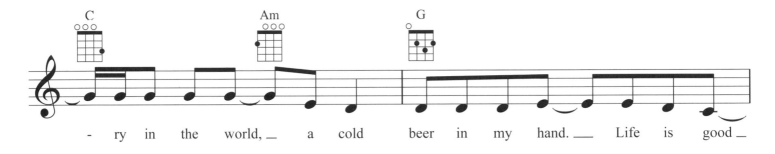

_____ to - day, life is good ___ to - day.

A - di - os and va - ya con

Chorus

Di - os,

yeah, I'm leav - in' G - A. _____
a long way ___ from G - A. _____
go - in' home ___ now to stay. _____

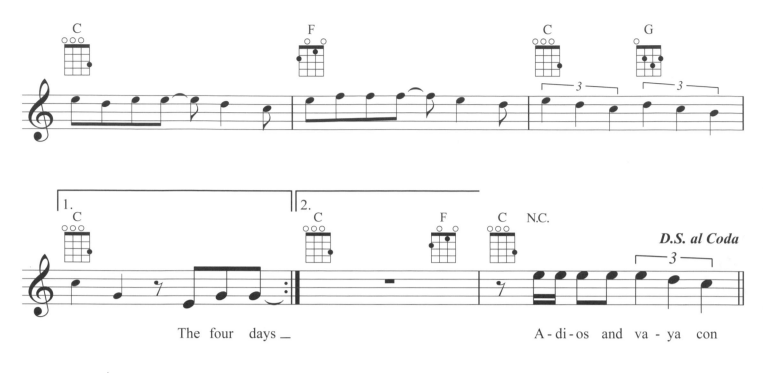

The four days _____

A - di - os and va - ya con

⊕ Coda

(Spoken:) Just gonna drive up by the lake   and   put   my

Outro

ass   in   a   lawn ____ chair,   toes ____ in   the   clay, ____ not   a   wor -

- ry   in   the   world, ___ a   P - B - R   on   the   way. ___ Life   is   good ____ to - day,

life   is   good ___ to - day.

Two Princes

Words and Music by Spin Doctors

First note

Verse
Moderately fast

1., 3. One, two princ-es kneel _ be-fore ____ you. That's what I said, _ now.
2. This one got a prince-ly rack - et. That's what I said, _ now.

Princ-es, princ-es who _ a-dore _ you. Just go a-head, _ now.
Got some big seal up-on ____ his jack - et. Ain't in his head, _ now.

One has dia-monds in ____ his pock - ets. That's some bread, _ now.
Mar-ry him, your fa-ther will _ con-done ____ you. How 'bout that, _ now? You

This one, he wants to buy _ you rock - ets. Ain't in his head, _ now.
mar-ry me, your fa-ther will _ dis-own ____ you. He'll eat his hat, _ now.

1. **Interlude**

Yeah, _____ yeah, yeah. _____ *(Vocal ad lib.)*

2., 3.
Pre-Chorus

Mar - ry him or mar - ry me. I'm _

_____ the one that loves you, ba - by. Can't you see? I ain't

got no fu - ture or a fam - 'ly tree, _____ but

I know what a prince and lov - er ought to be. _____

I know what a prince and lov - er ought to be. _____ Said,

Chorus

if you want to call ___ me, ba - by, just go a - head, __ now. And

if you'd like to tell ___ me may - be, just go a - head, __ now. And

if you wan-na buy ___ me flow - ers, just go a - head, __ now. And

if you'd like to talk ___ for ho - urs, just go a - head, __ now.

To Coda

D.C. al Coda
(take 2nd ending)

Coda

- urs, just go a - head, __ now.

Wake Me Up!

Words and Music by Aloe Blacc, Tim Bergling and Michael Einziger

They say I'm caught ___ up in ___ a dream. _____

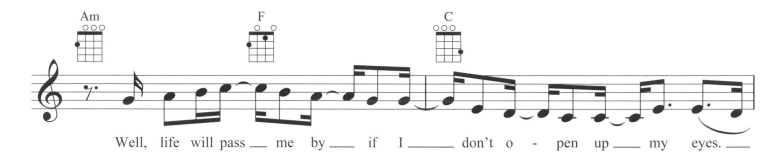

Well, life will pass ___ me by ___ if I ___ don't o - pen up ___ my eyes. ___

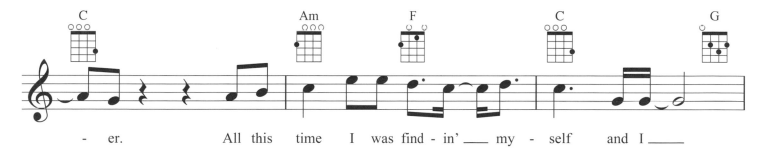

___ Well, that's fine by me. _____ So wake me

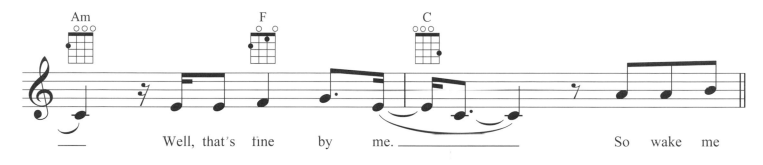

𝄋 Chorus

up when it's ___ all o - ver, when I'm wis - er and ___ I'm old -

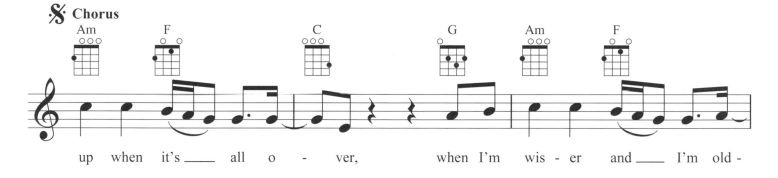

- er. All this time I was find - in' ___ my - self and I ___

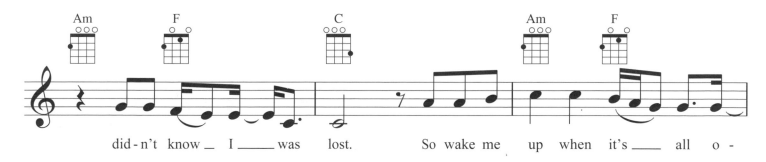

did - n't know ___ I ___ was lost. So wake me up when it's ___ all o -

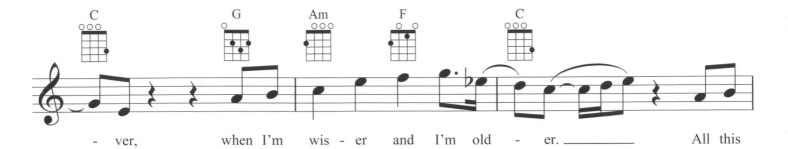

-ver, when I'm wis - er and I'm old - er. _____ All this

To Coda ⊕

time I was find - in' ___ my - self _____ { and I _____
{ and I, _____

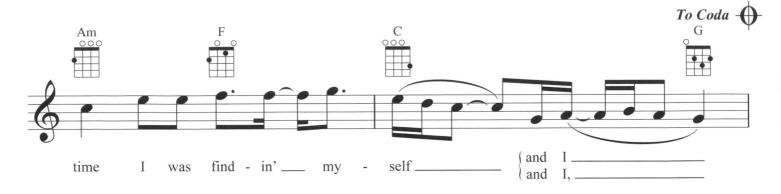

did - n't know I ___ was lost. _____

Verse

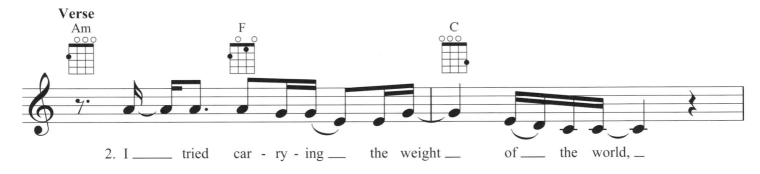

2. I ___ tried car - ry - ing ___ the weight ___ of ___ the world, ___

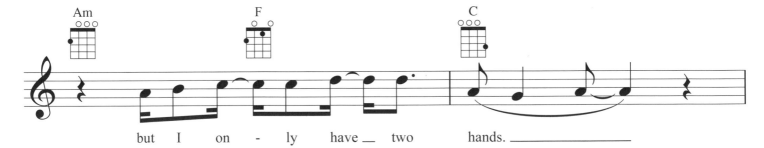

but I on - ly have ___ two hands. _____

Hope I get ___ a chance ___ to trav - el ___ the world, _____

but I don't have __ an - y plans. _____

Wish that I __ could stay __ for - ev - er this young. _____

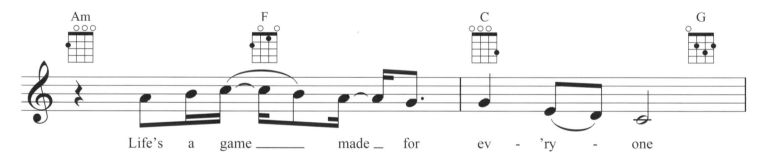

Not a - fraid __ to close __ my eyes. _____

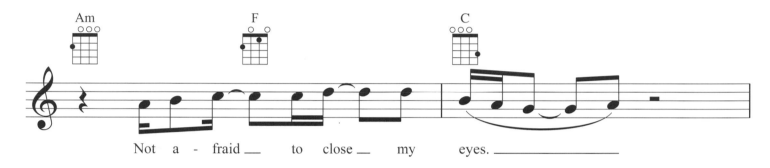

Life's a game _____ made _ for ev - 'ry - one

D.S. al Coda

and love is the prize. _____ So wake me

Coda

I did - n't know __ I __ was lost. _____

155

Wasting My Time

Words and Music by Danny Craig, Dallas Smith, Jeremy Hora and Dave Benedict

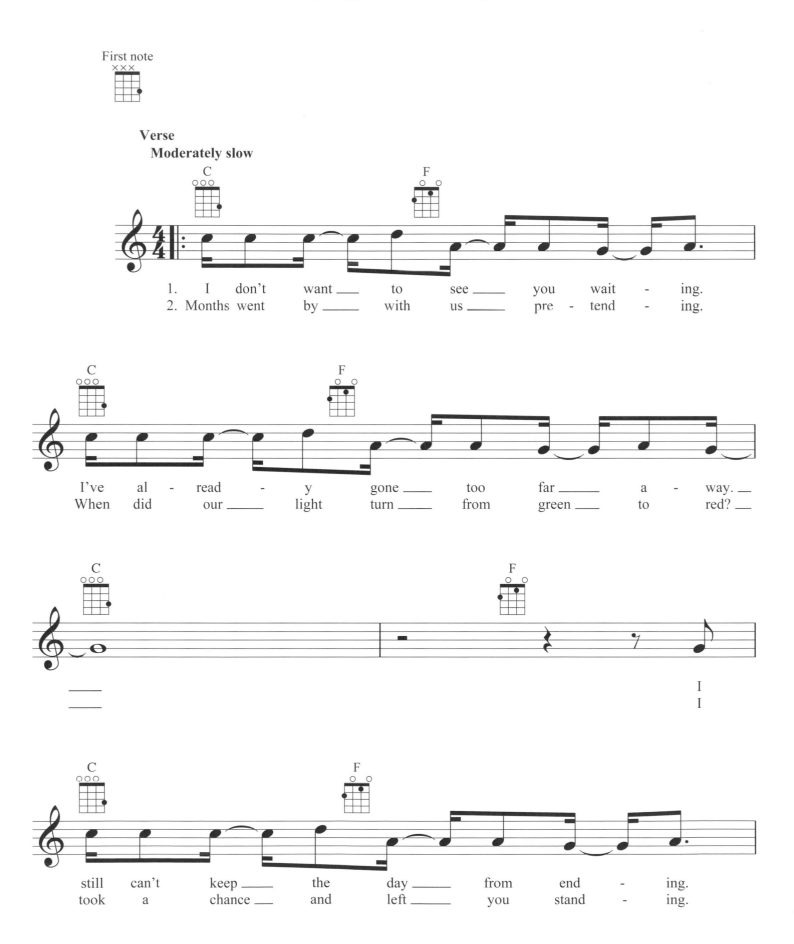

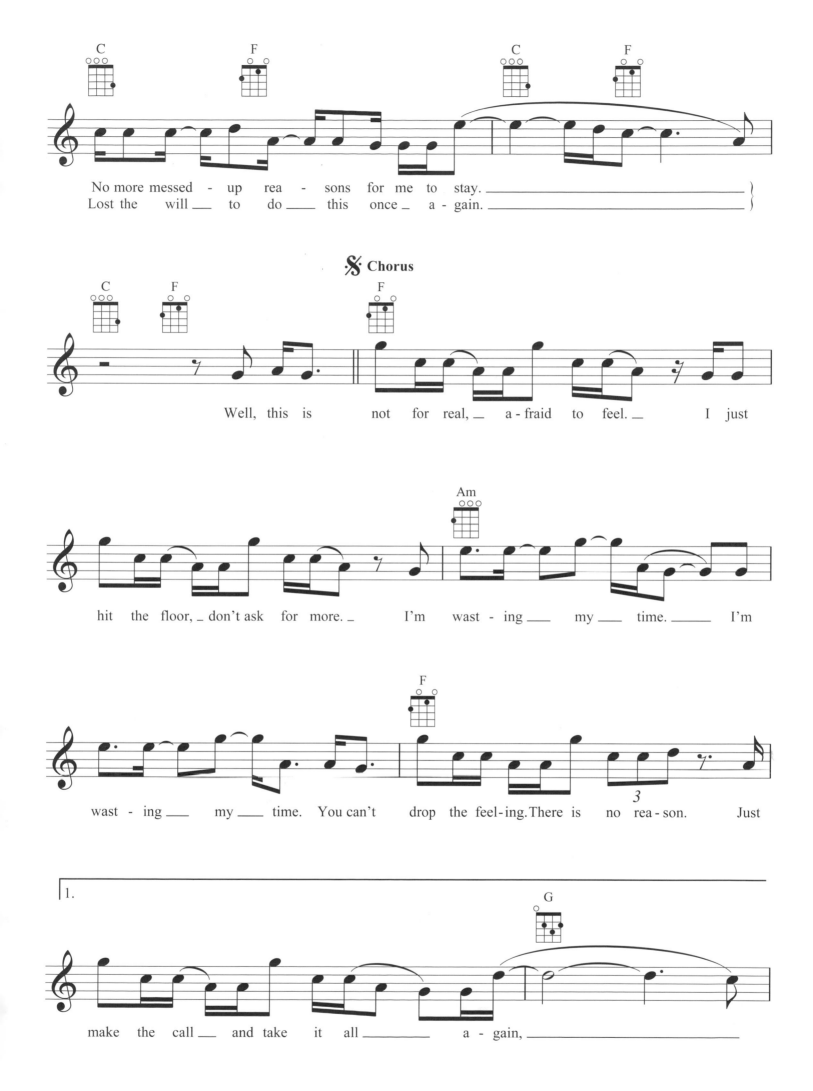

No more messed - up rea - sons for me to stay. _____
Lost the will ___ to do ___ this once ___ a - gain. _____

𝄋 Chorus

Well, this is not for real, ___ a - fraid to feel. ___ I just

hit the floor, ___ don't ask for more. ___ I'm wast - ing ___ my ___ time. _____ I'm

wast - ing ___ my ___ time. You can't drop the feel - ing. There is no rea - son. Just

1.

make the call ___ and take it all _____ a - gain, _____

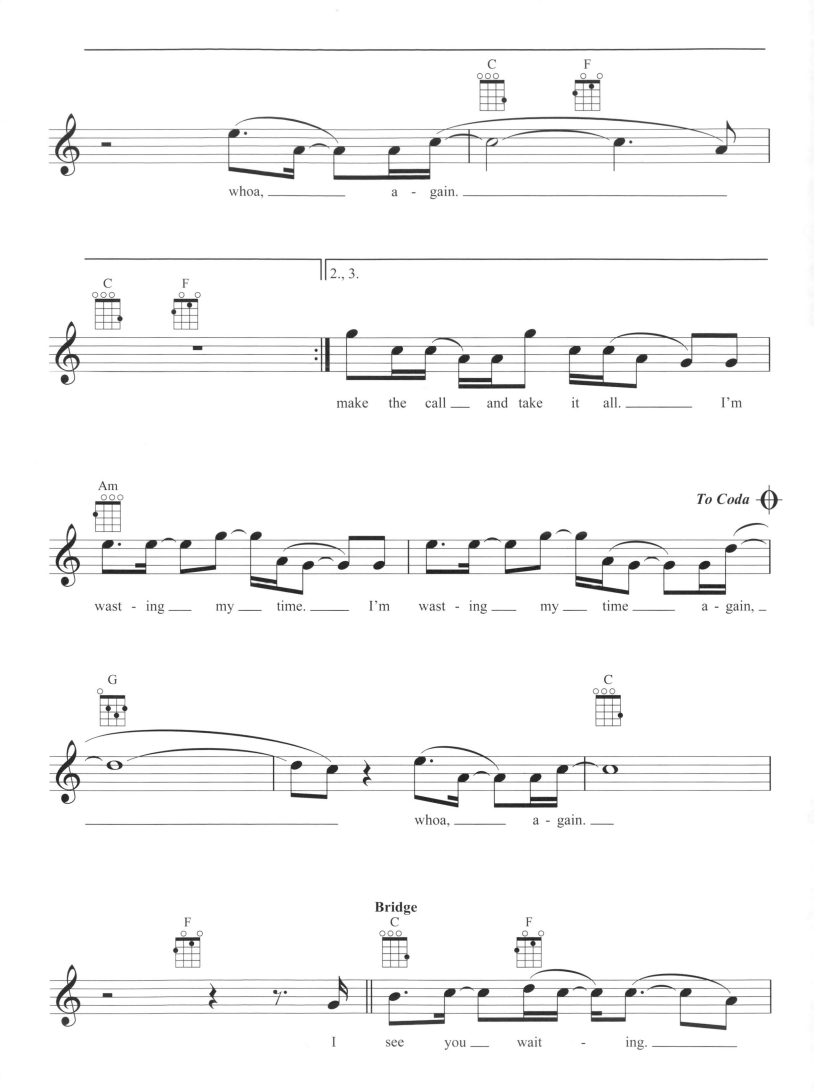

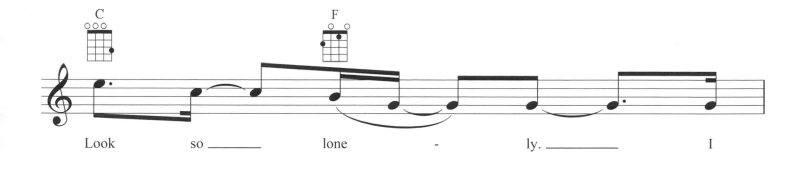

Look so _____ lone - ly. _____ I

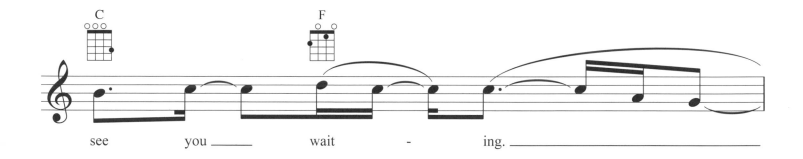

see you _____ wait - ing. _____

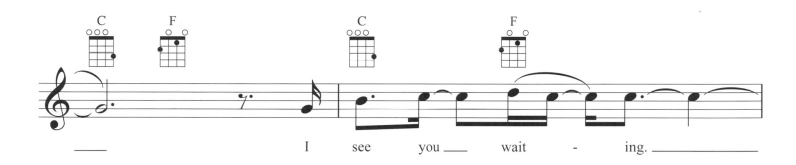

_____ I see you ___ wait - ing. _____

Coda

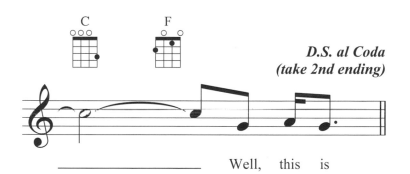

D.S. al Coda
(take 2nd ending)

_____ Well, this is

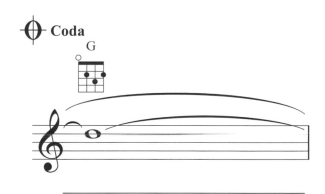

_____

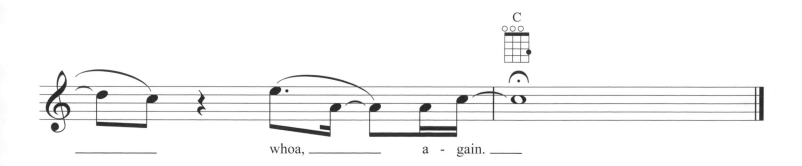

_____ whoa, _____ a - gain. ___

Where Were You
(When the World Stopped Turning)

Words and Music by Alan Jackson

First note

Verse
Moderately

1. Where were you when the world ____ stopped turn - in'
2. Where were you when the world ____ stopped turn - in'

that Sep - tem - ber day?   Out in the yard ____ with
that Sep - tem - ber day?   Teach - in' a class ____ full of

your wife and chil - dren   or work - in' on some stage ____ in L.
in - no - cent chil - dren   or driv - in' on some cold ____ in - ter -

A.?   Did you stand there in shock   at the
state?   Did you feel guilt - y   'cause ____

sight of that black smoke   ris - in' a - gainst that blue
you're a sur - vi - or?   In a crowd - ed room did you feel a -

Red, White and Blue ____ and he - roes who died just
think of to - mor - row, go out and buy you a

do - in' what ____ they do? Did you look up to heav - en for
gun? Did you turn off that vio - lent old

some kind ____ of an - swer and look at your - self ____ and
mov - ie _____ you're watch - in' and

Chorus

what real - ly mat - ters? I'm just a sing - er of ____

sim - ple songs. ____ I'm not a real po - lit - i - cal ____ man. I watch

C - N - N, ____ but I'm not ____ sure I can tell you the

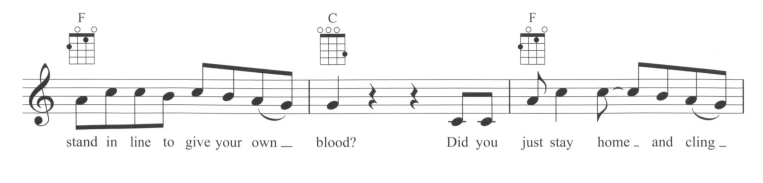

stand in line to give your own _ blood?   Did you   just stay   home _ and cling _

tight _ to your fam-'ly,   thank God you have some-bod-y   to   love? ____

Chorus

I'm just a sing-er of ____ sim-ple songs. _ I'm not a

real po-lit-i-cal _ man.   I watch   C - N - N, ___ but I'm not _

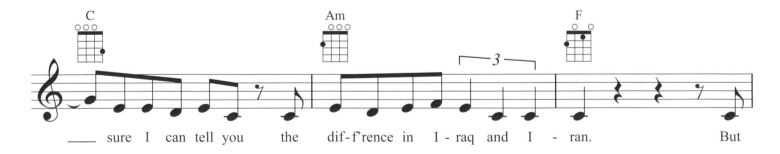

____ sure I can tell you   the   dif-f'rence in I - raq and I - ran.   But

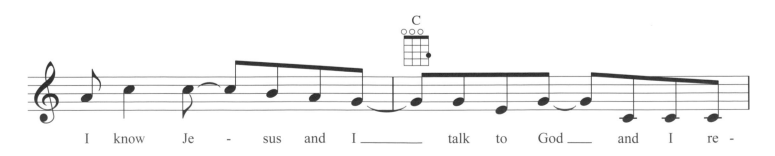

I know Je - sus and I _____ talk to God ___ and I re-

Who Do You Love

Words and Music by Steve Miller and Tim Davis

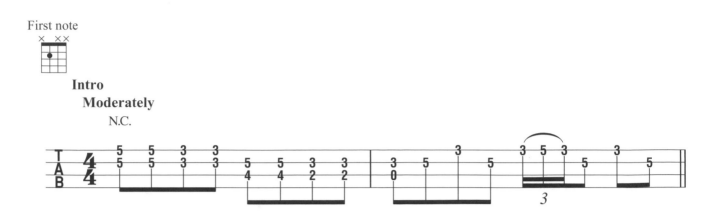

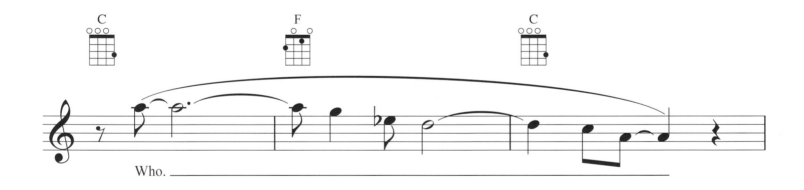

With or Without You

Words and Music by U2

First note

Intro
Moderately

C   G   Am

See the stone ___ set in your eyes, ___ see the thorn ___

F   C   G   Am

___ twist in your side. ___ I'll wait ___ for you. ___

Verse

F   C   G

1. Sleight of hand ___ and twist of fate, ___
2. Through the storm ___ we reach the shore. ___

Am   F   C

___ on a bed of nails ___ she makes me wait, ___ and I wait ___
You give it all, ___ but I want more, ___ and I'm wait -

G   Am   F

___ with - out ___ you, ___ with or with - out ___
- ing for ___ you, ___ with or with - out ___

You Raise Me Up

Words and Music by Brendan Graham and Rolf Lovland

UKULELE CHORD SONGBOOKS

This series features convenient 6" x 9" books with complete lyrics and chord symbols for dozens of great songs. Each song also includes chord grids at the top of every page and the first notes of the melody for easy reference.

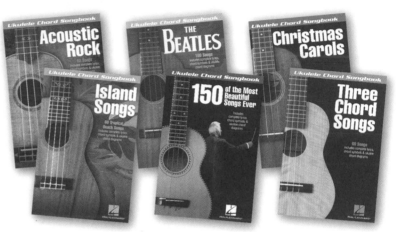

ACOUSTIC ROCK

60 tunes: American Pie • Band on the Run • Catch the Wind • Daydream • Every Rose Has Its Thorn • Hallelujah • Iris • More Than Words • Patience • The Sound of Silence • Space Oddity • Sweet Talkin' Woman • Wake up Little Susie • Who'll Stop the Rain • and more.
00702482 . . . . $15.99

THE BEATLES

100 favorites: Across the Universe • Carry That Weight • Dear Prudence • Good Day Sunshine • Here Comes the Sun • If I Fell • Love Me Do • Michelle • Ob-La-Di, Ob-La-Da • Revolution • Something • Ticket to Ride • We Can Work It Out • and many more.
00703065 . . . . $19.99

BEST SONGS EVER

70 songs: All I Ask of You • Bewitched • Edelweiss • Just the Way You Are • Let It Be • Memory • Moon River • Over the Rainbow • Someone to Watch over Me • Unchained Melody • You Are the Sunshine of My Life • You Raise Me Up • and more.
00117050 . . . . $16.99

CHILDREN'S SONGS

80 classics: Alphabet Song • "C" Is for Cookie • Do-Re-Mi • I'm Popeye the Sailor Man • Mickey Mouse March • Oh! Susanna • Polly Wolly Doodle • Puff the Magic Dragon • The Rainbow Connection • Sing • Three Little Fishies (Itty Bitty Poo) • and many more.
00702473 . . . . $17.99

CHRISTMAS CAROLS

75 favorites: Away in a Manger • Coventry Carol • The First Noel • Good King Wenceslas • Hark! the Herald Angels Sing • I Saw Three Ships • Joy to the World • O Little Town of Bethlehem • Still, Still, Still • Up on the Housetop • What Child Is This? • and more.
00702474 . . . . $14.99

CHRISTMAS SONGS

55 Christmas classics: Do They Know It's Christmas? • Frosty the Snow Man • Happy Xmas (War Is Over) • Jingle-Bell Rock • Little Saint Nick • The Most Wonderful Time of the Year • White Christmas • and more.
00101776 . . . . $14.99

ISLAND SONGS

60 beach party tunes: Blue Hawaii • Day-O (The Banana Boat Song) • Don't Worry, Be Happy • Island Girl • Kokomo • Lovely Hula Girl • Mele Kalikimaka • Red, Red Wine • Surfer Girl • Tiny Bubbles • Ukulele Lady • and many more.
00702471 . . . . $16.99

150 OF THE MOST BEAUTIFUL SONGS EVER

150 melodies: Always • Bewitched • Candle in the Wind • Endless Love • In the Still of the Night • Just the Way You Are • Memory • The Nearness of You • People • The Rainbow Connection • Smile • Unchained Melody • What a Wonderful World • Yesterday • and more.
00117051 . . . . $24.99

PETER, PAUL & MARY

Over 40 songs: And When I Die • Blowin' in the Wind • Goodnight, Irene • If I Had a Hammer (The Hammer Song) • Leaving on a Jet Plane • Puff the Magic Dragon • This Land Is Your Land • We Shall Overcome • Where Have All the Flowers Gone? • and more.
00121822 . . . . $14.99

THREE CHORD SONGS

60 songs: Bad Case of Loving You • Bang a Gong (Get It On) • Blue Suede Shoes • Cecilia • Get Back • Hound Dog • Kiss • Me and Bobby McGee • Not Fade Away • Rock This Town • Sweet Home Chicago • Twist and Shout • You Are My Sunshine • and more.
00702483 . . . . $15.99

TOP HITS

31 hits: The A Team • Born This Way • Forget You • Ho Hey • Jar of Hearts • Little Talks • Need You Now • Rolling in the Deep • Teenage Dream • Titanium • We Are Never Ever Getting Back Together • and more.
00115929 . . . . $14.99

Prices, contents, and availability subject to change without notice.

www.halleonard.com